# MOM,
# I Hate You!

# MOM,
# I Hate You!

**Children's Provocative Communication:**

**What It Means**

**and What to Do About It**

## Don Fleming, Ph.D.

**with Mark Ritts**

 THREE RIVERS PRESS
NEW YORK

Published by Three Rivers Press, New York, New York. Member of the Crown Publishing Group, a division of Random House, Inc.

www.randomhouse.com

THREE RIVERS PRESS and the Tugboat design are registered trademarks of Random House, Inc.

Printed in the United States of America

Design by Meryl Sussman Levavi/Digitext

Library of Congress Cataloging-in-Publication Data
Fleming, Don.
    Mom, I hate you! : children's provocative communication: what it means and what to do about it / Don Fleming, with Mark Ritts.
    Includes bibliographical references.
    1. Child psychology.   2. Interpersonal communication in children.   3. Communication in the family.   4. Parent and child.   5. Parenting.   I. Ritts, Mark.   II. Title.
    HQ772 .F54 2003
    649'.64—dc21                   2002011747

ISBN 0-609-80856-7

10  9  8  7  6  5  4  3  2  1

First Edition

*This book is dedicated to my wife,*
*Pamela Fleming.*
*A deeply sincere, caring, and kind human being,*
*she has made me a better person in so many ways.*
*I'm a lucky man to have her in my life.*

# Contents

# MOM,

# I Hate You!

# What Is Provocative Communication?

Your seven-year-old, hands on hips, declares defiantly, "You can't make me!" Your four-year-old tugs insistently on your sleeve, loudly whining "Mooooommmmmm!" while you're trying to chat with the important client you just bumped into at the supermarket. Your nine-year-old tries out the four-letter words he's learned at school on his three-year-old sister.

Before you conclude that your children have been sent to you as punishment for sins committed in a previous life, take heart. Such behavior, no matter how annoying or embarrassing, is completely normal. It's called "provocative communication," and it's a natural and (like it or not!) *necessary* part of growing up.

Provocative communication is any statement or nonverbal gesture from a child that appears rude, inappropriate, hurtful, or disrespectful. Some common examples are:

"Mom, I hate you!"
"I wish I never had a brother/sister!"
"I don't love you anymore!"
"You don't love me anymore!"
"I wish I/you were dead!"
"Shut up!"
"You can't make me!"
"You're stupid!"
"You never do anything for me!"
*"!%#@?@!!"*

In the following pages you'll learn how to decode provocative statements like these to reveal their underlying meanings and the important functions they perform in children's lives. You'll learn a variety of effective responses to provocative communication, keyed to specific situations and behavior patterns; responses that set appropriate limits on such behavior. You'll learn how to teach your children more effective ways to express themselves, ways that will give voice to their true feelings without causing conflict. And you'll learn the parameters of "normal" provocative communication and the threshold at which aggressive behavior enters the danger zone.

## A Look Back

In past generations, children were to be seen and not heard. They were expected to speak only when spoken to. Even mildly disrespectful behavior was considered intolerable and usually punished swiftly and severely—with a slap on the face, a spanking, or at the very least a harsh verbal lashing aimed at eliciting feelings of shame. There was a widespread double-standard in child-rearing practice. Parents could talk any way they wanted to their kids, but children had no such latitude. This do-as-I-say-not-as-I-do form of parenting is called "authoritarian discipline."

In such an atmosphere, children grew up without any sense of how to safely express their feelings. They thus tended to be less assertive, as well as less spontaneous and joyful. They also ceased to experience any comfort from the expression of emotion, squelching their strongest feelings just as their parents had squelched their impulses to express them.

Meanwhile, disciplinarian fathers and mothers felt they were doing a fine job of teaching their children self-control and good manners. Indeed, boys and girls were extraordinarily well-behaved by present-day standards, but it was at considerable cost to their emotional development and welfare.

Many of today's parents retain these disciplinarian attitudes, but there is also a widespread desire to understand what children are really trying to say when they express themselves provocatively. More parents than ever before are beginning to understand the importance of allowing children to give voice to their emotions, to let them out rather than bottle them up.

How, then, to exercise judicious control over children's provocative communication without squelching their emotional freedom and spontaneity? That is what this book is about.

## Preverbal Communication

How and when does provocative communication start? It begins with that first whack on the behind from the obstetrician! In translation, a newborn infant's cry means, "Ow! What'd you do that for? Cut it out! I'm cold! Put me back where you found me *right now*!"

Infants are expert at expressing displeasure. A baby's cry is preverbal communication at its most compelling. And it certainly provokes action on the part of adults—the immediate presentation of the mother's breast, for example— as well as a variety of strong emotions in the parent, from protectiveness to anxiety, frustration, and anger.

Crying is just the beginning, of course. Preverbal toddlers quickly expand their vocabulary of provocative communication to include physical acts like hitting, scratching, biting, and pulling hair. They have strong emotions, and they demonstrate them in the only ways they know how.

## No!

When small children begin to acquire language skills, their provocative vocabulary starts expanding by leaps and bounds. "No!" is often the first verbal provocative communication mothers and fathers receive from their kids. The little boy or girl who exclaims "No!" for the first time has recognized the remarkable power of words and is experimenting with that power. Who better to experiment on than Mommy and Daddy?

Preschoolers also learn to imitate the verbalizations

they hear around them. Some make monster sounds when they're angry (thanks to TV), or they repeat words and phrases other family members use. This imitative behavior often leads to eyebrow-raising expletives issuing from the mouths of three-year-olds. They don't really understand it as foul language, but only as "the thing Daddy says when he gets mad." Then, of course, there's whining, and the ultimate meltdown, the tantrum. This is the closest preschoolers come to all-out war, especially when it happens in a public place. Nonverbal provocative communication is still there at this age, too—and not just hitting and hair pulling, but more sophisticated gambits like going rigid and the dreaded "spaghetti legs."

By around the age of six, children's provocative communication can start to feel very personal—the severe look, the evil stare, hands on hips or folded in disgust. Parents sometimes find such dismissive gestures genuinely hurtful. By the age of eight, many children have added the "eye roll" to their provocative vocabularies, along with deep sighs—especially common when parents are attempting to teach children moral lessons. Still another provocative preadolescent behavior is the mumbled insult—the "I don't care" or "Oh, shut up" delivered *sotto voce*. Invariably, the parental response is an angry "What did you say?!" The child is smart enough not to repeat the words. "Nothing!" he or she insists. It's a frustrating exchange that's unproductive for all concerned.

## What to Do?

Although it may seem logical and natural to react strongly to children's provocative statements and gestures, the somewhat surprising reality is that most punitive or negative responses are ultimately ineffective. They don't succeed in changing the behavior "once and for all." More important, negative, punitive responses are frequently detrimental to the child because they foster guilt and shame; because they squelch emotion and inhibit the child's freedom of self-expression. In the chapters that follow, we will learn how to decode and decipher the feelings your child is expressing through provocative behavior. We'll also decode and decipher your own habitual responses to such behavior. Sometimes children's provocative behavior elicits an even worse counterassault from the parent. When caregivers begin to understand the *why* of their own feelings and actions, they're better able to change the *how* of their responses.

Look at it this way: Are your disciplinary interactions with your child producing the results you desire? If not, ask yourself whether your usual responses to provocation from your child are themselves provocative. Angry, punitive responses do not teach enduring lessons, lessons that your child willingly internalizes and lives by. More often, authoritarian discipline incites children merely to "humor" their parents cynically. It also tends to escalate provocative behavior because it models the very kind of aggressiveness you are trying to eliminate in your child.

## Powerful Emotions

Children have strong feelings and powerful impulses. They experience anger, frustration, hurt, disappointment, fear, jealousy—in short, all the emotions adults feel. But children are not necessarily equipped to express their feelings in the ways we deem appropriate. Further, children often feel powerless in a world governed by adults. And they react to this perceived tyranny by asserting themselves, sometimes very aggressively. As if all that weren't enough, children often feel overwhelmed by all the expectations adults place on them. "Do this!" "Do that!" "Don't do this!" "Don't do that!" They hear it all day. It's no wonder they can lose their patience! Unable to control their every impulse or thoughtfully regulate their reactions to the world around them, they "act out"; they react impulsively and openly in the only ways they know. They don't fully understand the impact of their words or actions; they just feel an overwhelming need to express themselves, no matter how it comes out.

## Different Types of Provocative Communication

Children's provocative communication can be broken down into a few broad categories:

**Persistent, Annoying Comments** Your child tugs on your sleeve, whining the same plea over and over: "I want some ice cream!" or "I want to go home!" or simply "Daaaad dyyyyy!" Young children have great difficulty deferring gratification. When they want something, they want it now, including their mom's or dad's complete attention. Parental reaction to such annoying behavior tends to escalate quickly from an offhanded "Shhh" to an angry "Stop that right this minute!!"

**Angry Comments** Kids get mad at all sorts of things—their parents, their siblings, their friends, their toys. They get mad at themselves, too. Often children's angry comments "cross the line" and elicit an even more irate response from a parent or sibling. The result is usually an intensification of the child's anger, making the situation worse for everyone.

**Bossy Comments** "Mommy, get me my milk!" "Put me down!" "That's mine! Don't touch it!" When very young children who are just learning to express themselves make bossy, hands-on-hips comments like these, grown-ups often laugh delightedly. Such dictatorial displays can seem very funny coming from a toddler. But later on, bossiness ceases to be a laughing matter, and most parents are no longer willing to tolerate it.

**Confusing Comments** These are statements that are provocative mainly because they're puzzling; they seem inappropriate, flying in the face of reason or the observable truth. A little girl comes home from nursery school and reports, "Miss Davis doesn't like me." A little boy says to his father at bedtime, "When you kiss me good night, I have bad dreams." The typical parental reaction to such statements is "Where did *that* come from? What's *that* all about?"

**Worrisome Comments** "I wish my sister would die." "I'm going to kill myself." "I hate my friends." Statements like these from very young children can send panicky parents in search of a psychologist. Most of the time, though, such comments are not indicative of any serious emotional problem. They simply reflect children's exaggerated reactions to daily life situations. Just the same, they do require appropriate responses.

The key for parents is to avoid *overreacting* to children's provocative communication, and to try instead to understand the powerful emotions behind the words. Young children are just learning self-expression, and frequently they don't really mean what they say or say what they mean. When parents learn how to guide their children toward clearer self-expression and a better understanding of their own feelings, communication becomes more rewarding and productive, and conflict is reduced. Parents and children alike feel better about themselves, and destructive feelings like guilt and shame are banished. Kids are very flexible. They want to learn, and they're good at it. It's never too late to teach your children—and yourself—more appropriate and mutually satisfying forms of interaction. Let's get started!

## A Word About How to Use This Book

At the risk of sounding facetious, the best way to use this book is to read it—all of it. *Take your time.* Reflect, in particular, on the things I have to say about discipline *without anger*. Practice the "scripts" I propose for interacting with your child. Examine your own habitual responses to your son or daughter as carefully as you analyze his or her behavior. The prescriptions I propose for controlling provocative communication in your home can be a considerable challenge for many people. But the potential rewards are incalculable.

This book does not offer a simple, three- or four-step program. In my view, parenting is far too complex and important a task to reduce to a few easy steps. Every child is different, both temperamentally and developmentally. Every parent is different, too, and so is every household. One size simply doesn't fit all. So I will describe a variety of responses to provocative behavior tailored to different kinds of kids and circumstances.

*(continued)*

(continued)

Finally, this book focuses on preadolescent children. Its basic lessons can be applied with great effectiveness to teenagers, but the case histories and other illustrations I have chosen throughout involve kids from three or four to eleven or twelve years of age.

# Provocative Communication and Your Child's Development

So, children are born with the ability to communicate provocatively. Crying works beautifully. It summons Mommy and Daddy. It causes holding and cuddling and playing. It gets diapers changed. It brings food. What else is there?!

Of course, as time passes and children begin to acquire language skills, provocative communication becomes more and more varied and sophisticated—from the tantrum-prone twos, to the more aggressive and bossy fours, to the argumentative sixes, to the smart-ass nines and tens, to the all-of-the-above adolescent years. The bottom line is that provocative communication is a fundamental part of the human apparatus for coping with life. The extent to which we control our natural provocative urges is a function of age and maturity. Young children tend to "let it all hang out," so they dive right in and make highly provocative statements that we grown-ups might be a little more likely to keep to ourselves.

## The Need for Independence

Children speak provocatively out of a growing need for independence and identity. The little girl who exclaims "You can't make me!" or even simply "No, I won't!" is trying to assert her separateness. She is saying, "I'm *me*, and you're *you*! Let me be *me*!" Kids are small, and they *feel* small. Adults run their lives for them. They're hemmed in on all sides by rules and prohibitions. Stretching the limits makes them feel bigger and more important. Even though they have no serious desire to leave the nest, they're flexing the muscles they'll one day use to go off on their own.

## Control

Provocative communication is also a logical side effect of children's quests to exert some control over their ever-expanding worlds. Kids experience a lot of frustration. Their abilities are limited, and they know it. They wish they could reach the cookie jar. They wish they could be stronger than their big brother or sister. They wish for everything they know they can't have. They want control so badly that they often refuse help even when they know they need it, or insist on doing something their own way even when they're fully aware that doing it Mom's or Dad's way is easier. Unfortunately, try as they may, kids invariably fail to get as much control as they would like, and the resulting frustration comes out in the form of provocative, aggressive communication.

## Egocentricity

Young children are very egocentric—that is, they see themselves as the center of the world. Other people and things are interesting to them only insofar as they can fulfill personal needs. This egocentricity (which isn't "bad," merely normal) causes a shortage of empathy for others—especially for Mom and Dad, because they are usually the most reliable need-fillers. When parents fail to deliver the goods, no matter what the reason, the child bitterly resents it and does not hesitate to tell them so.

Further, children want what they want when they want it! They have great difficulty deferring gratification. When their parents insist on delay, provocative responses are often the result—"You never do anything for me!" "I always have to wait for everything!" or the old standby, usually repeated until the parent is ready to scream: *"Whyyyyyy?!"*

## Types of Development

Children grow in a variety of ways. For one thing, they get bigger. They also grow cognitively, socially, emotionally, and sexually. Provocative communication is an outgrowth of each of these growth categories. In other words, provocative communication is stimulated by children's cognitive development, emotional development, social development, and so forth. Let's look at them one at a time. . . .

## Provocative Communication and Cognitive Development

*Cognitive development* is the process of learning, the process of acquiring skills, knowledge, and judgment. Cognitive abilities include everything from knowing how to play patty-cake, to knowing the ABC's, to knowing not to step off a cliff. Children begin to develop cognitively from the moment they are born, and we are all still acquiring cognitive skills to one degree or another until the day we die. Very young children find learning exciting and fun. Witness the joy on the face of a three- or four-year-old who has just learned how to form a letter or numeral with a crayon. As long as preschoolers aren't pressured to learn too much too soon, they will usually display a natural, cheerful desire to acquire new knowledge and skills. As they get older, however, they are presented with more and more challenging learning tasks, especially at school. They must concentrate and focus; they must absorb and remember more. With all this responsibility comes greater potential for frustration and confusion. And because kids want independence and control, they also want to be right. Being wrong constitutes a loss of control. So children tend to become defensive when they're shown to be wrong. Frustration, confusion, defensiveness—it all means greater potential for provocative communication directed at parents, teachers, and peers.

"I don't want to do my homework now!"

"I'm not doing it again! It's good enough!"

"I *never* get to have any *fun*!"

"We don't have to know that!"

"I *know*! I *know*!"

"You don't know anything, Mom!"

Does any of this sound familiar? Most parents of elementary school students have heard remarks like these again and again. But here's the rub: Your child's frustration, confusion, and defensiveness aren't the only culprits. Unfortunately, there's a strong likelihood that you are, too.

Most mothers and fathers tend to react in kind to their children's provocative statements—that is, they communicate provocatively right back. They are, themselves, frustrated over their kids' attitudes and confused about what to do. Rather than accepting their children's normal struggles with their schoolwork and other responsibilities, they are often impatient or critical. The result is that the child's unpleasant behavior is not discouraged, but rather, perpetuated. Does the following interaction seem vaguely familiar?

> A nine-year-old boy expresses an incorrect understanding of some school material. "Henry Hudson discovered America, not Christopher Columbus," he says to his mother. "Henry Hudson?! Where'd you get *that* idea?!" she replies in an incredulous tone. "In school, in case you didn't know it," he replies testily. "Watch your mouth!" she retorts.

Here the problem is not really with the boy. Early American explorers are new to nine-year-olds. It's normal for them to misunderstand some of the things they're taught. The mother's impatient, implicitly critical reaction hurt the child's feelings. He felt threatened and defensive—a completely normal reaction for a nine-year-old. The result was a testy, provocative retort, which was answered by an equally provocative admonition from the mother. Had the parent been more patient and accepting of the child's misunderstanding, the provocative communication would probably never have occurred.

Let's look at another example of a parent's unwitting stimulation of provocative interaction:

An eight-year-old girl asks her father for help with her math for the third night in a row. "You know, if you keep asking me for help with your schoolwork, you'll never be able to do anything on your own!" he declares. She leaves the room, mumbling, "You don't know anything, anyway." "Hey!" he exclaims. "I heard that!"

Again, the father responded to his daughter's request for help with criticism. She reacted defensively/provocatively. Had the father adopted a more patient strategy for weaning his daughter from his assistance, the unpleasant aspects of the exchange could have been avoided.

As these paragraphs suggest, this is not a book about ill-behaved kids and how their blameless parents can discipline them. The people children live with—their mothers and fathers and other caregivers—are the most prominent behavioral examples in their young lives. Kids model themselves after the adults who raise them. Dealing with all our children's behavior requires not only a close look at *them*, but a close look at *ourselves* as well.

## Things to Remember About Provocative Communication and Your Child's Cognitive Development

◆ When children are two to four years old, the *correctness* of their freely associated thoughts and ideas is not particularly important. It's better to encourage them to think without restriction, even when they've "got it all wrong," than to correct them all the time. Let their imaginations soar; resist the temptation to bring them down to earth!

(continued)

(continued)

♦ When kids have reached an age where they really need to have the right answers, as with schoolwork, try to be calm, supportive, and patient. Suggest alternative answers to your child: "Could this be the right answer to the problem? How about this?" This helps the child feel that he or she is still actively participating in the search for the right answer without completely relinquishing control to the parent. The result: a more friendly and productive interaction, as well as better retention of the correct answer by the child.

♦ Remember, when your child is being provocative about schoolwork, it's usually best to resist immediate "engagement." If you have to, leave the room for a minute or two to collect yourself and decide how best to proceed calmly. Don't return with eyes blazing and teeth bared! Better to defer action than to add fuel to the fire!

## Provocative Communication and Social Development

As we all know, children are born uncivilized. Infants have no social skills. If they did, they'd refrain from soiling their diapers and always smile at their grandparents.

Social skills are learned—from parents, siblings, peers, and general observation of the world. It's not an easy task. Children take considerable time to refine their behavior. It takes years of practice, exposure to a broad variety of social experiences, and much experimentation. Most adults would admit that they are still learning how to get along with other people.

Children's social development encompasses a broad

variety of social interactions that can generate provocative feelings and behavior. Kids are often the victims of teasing and rejection. They have disagreements at play and in the classroom. Young children's natural inclinations to be controlling and bossy can get them into social scrapes. They often experience disappointment in their interactions with family and friends. They also face frequent situations in which they must decide quickly whether to retreat or stand their ground.

Why do these situations elicit so much provocative behavior in kids? Because their behavioral vocabulary is limited and less nuanced than an adult's. Their feelings tend to be strong and unambiguous. They are entertained or bored, content or angry. Adult behavior has subtle variations. Childish behavior is all about extremes. Further, children's expressive vocabulary is limited and far less nuanced than an adult's, too. So we have a situation that is volatile on two counts: extreme feelings that can only be expressed in extreme ways. This is why kids are frequently heard making statements that are jarring in their cruelty:

> "I hate you!"
> "Nobody likes you!"
> "You're ugly!"
> "You're so stupid!"

Kids lack the subtlety to say "I sometimes find this particular aspect of your behavior irritating." Instead, they just blurt out something along the lines of "You suck!"

A little earlier we discussed how children desire independence and control over their lives. We also saw that being wrong constitutes a loss of that control. Embarrassment is a big issue for kids. It's a form of being wrong, and it occurs frequently in the course of children's social interactions.

Apart from being a blow to self-esteem, embarrassment also invites teasing—adding insult to injury. Most of us can remember more than one highly embarrassing moment in our childhoods: the tray full of food dropped in the school cafeteria (followed, of course, by tumultuous applause), the mismatched shoes or socks, the bad haircut, the humiliating scolding by an adult in front of peers. When children are embarrassed, they often lash out defensively:

> Nine-year-old Matthew's father discovers him pushing a friend around in the backyard. "Matthew!" he exclaims. "Stop picking on Joel! You're being a brat!" Matthew replies rudely, "I can do what I want with him! He's *my* friend!"

Matthew was embarrassed in front of his playmate, so he lost his temper with his dad. His aggressive retort was a way of regaining the "face" he lost when his father humiliated him with a public scolding.

> Maria, eight, fails a quiz at school. A classmate, Carl, announces this to a large group of children at recess, declaring Maria stupid. Maria comes home, kicks her little brother, and exclaims "Leave me alone!" when her bewildered mother offers her a snack.

Again, the provocative behavior is the result of embarrassment and humiliation in front of peers. Maria expressed her upset in the only ways she knew how.

Provocative communication is also frequently a result of imitation. Children can form very strong attachments to peers. "Best friends" can be all but inseparable.

When one such best friend has a provocative bent, for

whatever reason, the second often adopts the same behavior pattern.

> Jessica has a favorite put-down. "He's a *reeetard*!" she loves to say. Her best friend, Suzanna, never used to say mean things (according to her mom). But now, it's a rare day when Suzanna doesn't declare someone "a *reeetard*!"

Jessica may have learned the expression from an older brother or sister. Whatever its source, it now provides a means for both Jessica and Suzanna to feel superior to others—to feel more powerful—and as we've said, children want power.

Still another source of provocative communication in children is their recurrent decision-making over when to hold their ground and when to back down. The child who has been called a name by a peer has two choices: reciprocate, thereby risking an escalation of the conflict, or retreat, thereby risking public humiliation. Neither option is very attractive.

> At recess, Douglas calls Jason an idiot. Jason decides that he prefers prolonging the battle to being perceived by his peers as a pushover. So he stands his ground and retaliates by calling Douglas a jerk. "You're ugly, too!" he adds. A fight ensues, broken up by their fifth-grade teacher. Jason is secretly grateful for the intervention, but even more grateful that his public image is intact. Had the fight continued, he might have lost. He might even have cried, which would have exposed him to one of the greatest humiliations of all: being called a crybaby.

Children's social development is a rocky road that they must negotiate as best they can with limited resources. Their self-awareness is minimal; their understanding of the roots of other people's behavior is sketchy at best; their arsenal of responses to life's demands is meager. So it's no wonder they lash out, that they so quickly resort to provocative communication under stress.

## Things to Remember About Provocative Communication and Your Child's Social Development

♦ Children's behavior in social situations can improve of its own accord with maturity. But the process is sped up when parents set good examples and avoid stimulating and perpetuating aggressive behavior, however unwittingly

♦ When your child behaves inappropriately with peers, take him or her aside to discuss it. This avoids humiliating the child in front of others, which often stimulates further outbursts.

♦ When parents assiduously model nonprovocative forms of communication, even in stressful situations, children learn to manage and control their aggressive inclinations much sooner.

♦ Avoid excessive lecturing and moralizing to your children. It invites provocative reactions. Your kids will see it as intrusive and tiresome and will almost certainly reject your advice.

♦ Remember that growing up can be hard, painful work. Peers can be cruel and unforgiving. Children deserve your patience and empathy as they struggle to mature socially.

♦ Remember, too, that your child's outbursts can mask deeper emotions—as in the example above about Maria,

(continued)

(continued)

who kicked her brother because she failed a school quiz. Provocative communication may be the outward manifestation of hidden feelings of rejection, jealousy, or other such negative emotions. In a later chapter, we'll discuss how to get to the bottom of provocative communication and reveal its sometimes hidden roots.

## Provocative Communication and Emotional Development

As children grow emotionally and learn new ways to express themselves, their provocative vocabulary changes. Often, children speak provocatively without fully understanding the severity or impact of their words. It's simply because they don't comprehend their own feelings or know quite what to do with them. With the passage of years, and with thoughtful parental guidance, kids learn to understand their emotions more deeply and express them in healthier ways.

Infants and preverbal toddlers are essentially "open books." When they're unhappy, they cry or fuss. It's up to the caregivers to figure out what's upsetting them. Preverbal power struggles can also take the form of the dreaded tantrum, the doubly dreaded public tantrum, and a host of other aggressive gestures like biting, scratching, hitting, and hair pulling.

When children acquire language, their provocative arsenal becomes far more varied. Preschool children often express their provocative feelings through fantasy.

Michael, age four, has an imaginary friend named Petey. One day, Michael approaches his father in the living room and whispers, "Petey says if you don't take me to the store with you, he's going to beat you up!"

Michael is letting Petey do the dirty work for him. Of course, it's Michael, not Petey, who is threatening Dad with retribution. What Michael wants, as we've seen in previous examples, is power—power over his father. Two-, three-, and four-year-olds work out many of their hostilities, fears, and conflicts in similar fashion, exercising their fertile imaginations and fantasizing about what they wish were true, or not true, in their lives.

Laura, age three, is observed by her mother talking to her stuffed dog. "My skin is stronger than your teeth," she says to the little animal. "It doesn't even hurt if you bite me."

Laura is actually concerned about the next-door neighbors' aggressively playful collie. She quiets her fears by imagining the absence of any real threat.

Miguel, four, loves to wear the superhero cape his grandmother made for him. "I have super powers!" he shouts at his older brother, striking a threatening pose. "I can fly and you can't! Ha!" He then takes off with a *whoosh* (a sound effect he produces with his mouth). This drives his big brother crazy.

Miguel is getting a lot out of this provocative gambit. He is acting out his desire to be more powerful than his big brother. He also knows that this annoys his big brother, which is, itself, a form of power over the older boy. So Miguel is not only fantasizing, he's actually turning his fantasy into reality! This brings us to another dimension of the emotional life of young children: grandiosity. Kids want control—over their parents, over their siblings and playmates, over their lives in general—and they use their imaginations to paint grandiose portraits of themselves in their own minds. They fantasize about being superheroes, celebrated ballerinas, race car drivers, astronauts, princesses, Olympic athletes. All of these icons represent mastery, control, and power. Grandiose fantasies have an important function in young lives. As children imagine themselves becoming anyone they want—the best of the best, the most attractive, the most talented, the most admired—they are developing their self-esteem and cultivating hopeful, optimistic feelings about their lives. We all need that, and children are no exception. As we saw in the "Miguel" example above, grandiosity can also take provocative forms. When a small child imagines himself to be powerful enough to take on an older brother in hand-to-hand combat and win by a knockout, he is dealing emotionally with sibling rivalry and working through his fears and resentments. In short, he's growing.

By the time children reach school age, they have usually begun to resolve conflict more directly and efficiently through verbal interaction with family members and friends. When preschoolers have learned at home that it's all right to express their feelings, even when those feelings are provocative, they progress more rapidly and easily toward resolving conflict through discussion and cooperative problem-solving. In the coming chapters, we'll learn how to make this happen.

## Things to Remember About Provocative Communication and Your Child's Emotional Development

- ◆ Provocative communication is, by definition, emotional, so your child's emotional development is most often the source of aggressive words and deeds. Usually, it's all about power. Your kids need you, and they know it. But on another level, they wish they didn't, because their need for you means they're not in control. The result is a constant push-pull, a constant ambivalence that encourages provocative outbursts.
- ◆ Your job as a parent or other caregiver is to place appropriate boundaries on provocative communication—boundaries that set limits without unduly squelching the freedom to express emotion.
- ◆ On occasion, a child's behavior can seem so outlandishly awful that one wonders if an exorcism is in order. When this happens, fear not! You're probably just experiencing your child at his or her provocative best. Remember, adults have occasional major flare-ups, too!
- ◆ The emotional sector of children's development has the power to produce the most extreme and primitive responses in the parent. It is the area in which parental overreaction is most common and the most difficult to control.

## Provocative Communication and Sexual Development

Children are already beginning to develop a sexual identity by the time they're three or four. They're beginning to recognize that there are differences between girls and boys, and they're starting to see themselves clearly as one or the other.

They're also becoming curious about their body processes and sexual parts—and about their parents' and siblings' as well. They adopt whatever words they have become familiar with to discuss these matters—poop, peepee, penis, vagina, and so forth—and use them with great joy and repetitiveness. Parents face a dilemma here. If they do not limit their small child's use of these words, they risk having a memorably embarrassing moment at the next church supper. If, on the other hand, they try to discourage their child from saying such things, they risk turning the words into all-the-more-tempting "forbidden fruit." A child who sees that his parents are upset by a particular word will be more likely to use it provocatively. More on this in later chapters.

As children outgrow "baby words" for bodily functions and sexual matters, the new words they begin to use are no longer cute, but commonly considered profane. They pick them up from older siblings, from classmates, from the media, and from parents who don't watch their language sufficiently around the house. Often, eight- to ten-year-olds don't fully comprehend what all these words mean. But they are thoroughly familiar with the effect they have on others—their apparent power and eloquence in expressing disapproval and anger. Kids also recognize that four-letter expletives are "grown-up words," which makes them all the more attractive.

Most often, school-age children use scatological and sexual profanity among themselves. They have learned the hard way that cursing around parents and teachers gets them into trouble. But privately, it is an expression of power and sexual identity, especially for boys. When parents begin to see their children's use of provocatively graphic or sexual language as a normal, albeit troublesome, part of growing up, they can begin to deal with it more effectively and constructively. Kids employ profanity in the same way most adults do—to help express their strongest feelings. However, children need to learn from their parents and other caregivers appropriate limits on the use of these words and expressions.

## Things to Remember About Provocative Communication and Your Child's Sexual Development

♦ Young children's fascination with bodily functions and their own and other people's sexual parts is normal and not a precursor of excessive sexual preoccupation in adolescence or adulthood. If your children use scatological or sexual imagery to provoke you, rest assured that it's a common phenomenon. That doesn't mean you should ignore it, but it does mean there's rarely cause for alarm

♦ Remember your own childhood. You can probably recollect some of your own early sexual feelings, secrets, and preoccupations. Your children are no different. Have patience!

## Provocative Communication and Physical Development

Finally, children's physical size and abilities can illicit all sorts of provocative behavior. As boys and girls grow taller, they are often emboldened. They become more willing to confront parents, teachers, and other authority figures aggressively. However, the overlarge and awkward child may behave provocatively not out of simple boldness but out of a desire to preserve self-esteem.

Preschool children are fairly oblivious to differences in

physical stature and ability among their peers. But by the time kids reach ages eight or nine, they have become quite aware of where they stand in the pecking order. Third- and fourth-graders who are larger, smaller, fatter, or thinner than their peers know it only too well. They are often subjected to teasing and may fight back, in which case the provocative behavior is direct and immediate. Other children may withdraw socially as a result of teasing and take their aggressions out indirectly on parents or siblings. For school-age boys, athletic skills have traditionally been a focal point of physical awareness. For girls, physical appearance is a more dominant standard. Each can be a breeding ground for provocative communication.

### Things to Remember About Provocative Communication and Your Child's Physical Development

- School-age boys and girls quickly become aware of how their physical stature and prowess compares to that of their peers. The verdict they reach about themselves in that regard can have a powerful effect on their provocative communication.
- Increasing physical size can have a positive effect in reducing a child's desire to prove him- or herself. It can also have a negative effect by emboldening a child to be more confrontational.
- When children perceive themselves to be *too* anything in regard to physical stature—too fat, too thin, too tall, too short—provocative behavior can be the result. It may take the form of direct confrontation with children

(continued)

(continued)

who tease them, or indirect "acting-out" with parents, siblings, teachers, or peers.
◆ Children's self-analysis of their physical attributes can be very unforgiving and nitpicky. A nine-year-old can become morose and argumentative for days over a private verdict on ear size or hair color.

The bottom line is that every aspect of childhood development—cognitive, social, emotional, sexual, physical—has a provocative side, a constantly simmering provocative potential. Children need to work through their feelings of resentment, fear, hostility, disappointment, anger, and jealousy as they search for who they are and how they fit into the world. It's a process that really never ends, and as we'll continue to see throughout this book, it begins early!

# 3

# Decoding the Meaning Behind Children's Words

In this chapter we'll learn how to identify patterns in your child's provocative communication, and we'll explore ways to discern the meanings behind provocative words and behavior. Many of the things your child says and does, especially when he or she is angry or frustrated, require decoding, because children often do not respond to the world in ways an adult would consider logical and appropriate. They tend to "overreact" in the eyes of grown-ups. They exhibit delayed reactions, suddenly venting feelings about events that occurred days or even weeks in the past. They often "project" their feelings of unhappiness, taking them out on unsuspecting parents, siblings, and friends. To make matters even worse, grown-ups can have considerable difficulty seeing an issue or event from a child's point of view.

## The Feelings Behind the Words

Not only do the things children say frequently fail to convey their true feelings, but often kids simply don't know how to express what's on their minds without being provocative. Decoding provocative words and behavior usually uncovers one or more of just a few fundamental, negative feelings kids commonly experience:

- ◆ *Feeling "left out"*—Sometimes this has to do with frustration at being unable to participate in the activities of older siblings and grown-ups. Often it will surface with remarks like "Everybody hates me" or "Nobody wants to play with me" or "I don't have any friends." Parents generally respond to such statements in one of two ways: they either disbelieve and fail to validate them, saying things like "That's not true, honey," or they become overly concerned.

- ◆ *Embarrassment*—Kids are extremely prone to embarrassment, especially in front of their peers. When parents embarrass their children by scolding them in front of friends or by revealing something their children consider private, extremely provocative reactions can ensue—from "Shut up!" and "I hate you!" to looks that could kill.

- ◆ *Hurt feelings*—When children's feelings are hurt by something another child, or an adult, has said to them, they sometimes withdraw emotionally. In other instances they may react in openly hostile, aggressive ways. Hurt feelings have a parallel in feeling threatened, as when a child observes a parent's affectionate interaction with a sibling, a friend, or even a pet, and complains, "You love him/her more than you love me!"

◆ *Disappointment*—Because children are very self-involved, they have great difficulty tolerating disappointment. Parents' broken promises can elicit provocative reactions like "You never do anything for me!" and "I wish you weren't my mommy and daddy!"

◆ *Defeat*—As discussed, kids want power. Some parents indulge their children's delight in winning by intentionally losing game after game of Old Maid or Chutes and Ladders. Others believe that kids need to face life just as it is and never allow them an unearned victory. This can lead to provocative behavior—in particular, insistence on starting a game over when an opponent takes an early lead. But the fact remains that in their day-to-day lives, boys and girls suffer many defeats, large and small. These failures can bring on provocative remarks like "I don't want to play with you anymore!" and "You cheat!"

◆ *Not getting one's way*—Again, because children are very self-absorbed, they react negatively to being overruled. They want what they want when they want it. It's all a natural part of the growth process, but the result is provocative comments like "You can't make me!" and "I can if I want to!"

Keep the feelings described above in mind as you consider the following examples of decoding:

"No more candy now, Melissa," a mom says to her five-year-old. "You never let me have *anything*!" Melissa retorts, and stomps out of the room.

*What Melissa might have said if she could:* "It's really hard for me when I don't get my way, Mommy!"

Dad cancels a long-anticipated weekend trip to the zoo with Jonathan, age seven. Three days later, Uncle Don takes the boy to the movies. "I wish Uncle Don was my dad and not you," Jonathan suddenly tells his perplexed father the next day.

*What Jonathan might have said if he could:* "Daddy, when you disappoint me, I may not show it right away, but I get very upset. Uncle Don didn't disappoint me yesterday, so I wish you were more like him!"

Marc, age nine, comes home from a Little League game that his team lost, 24 to 3. He pulls a toy out of his little sister's hands and flings it under the sofa. "Mommieeeee!" she screams. "Shut up, crybaby," he sneers as he disappears into his room, slamming the door behind him.

*What Marc might have said if he could:* "It's really hard for me to lose, Sis. It makes me feel mad, bad, and sad, and I'm taking all my unhappy feelings out on you! I wish I could cry, too, but that would make *me* a crybaby, which is even worse!"

Dealing effectively with children's provocative communication requires a real effort to understand how their developing minds process information and how they are reacting emotionally to the complicated world around them—a world with which they have had very limited experience. Sometimes the decoding process is simple; other times it can be surprisingly difficult. But an important key to controlling children's provocative communication lies in responding not so much to the words as to the meanings behind them. Consider the following exchange:

A second-grader comes home and is confronted by his mother. "Stevie," she says, "your teacher called me today and told me you've been acting silly in class and making it hard for the other children to do their work." "Mom, you're getting very old! You have a lot of wrinkles!" Stevie replies. "Don't you talk to me like that!" his mother scolds.

On its surface, the conversation is very disjointed. Mom's wrinkles have nothing to do with a call from the teacher. But the meaning behind the words is quite clear: Stevie didn't want to talk about his behavior in school. Why? For the simple reason that getting into trouble feels bad. So he tried to remove the focus from himself by radically changing the subject. Unfortunately, his mother took the bait and responded to the provocative remark about her age. She responded to *the words*, not to the meaning *behind* them. The result is an even more irritated mother and an abashed and now probably less-communicative-than-ever boy.

So how might the mother have responded to the meaning behind the words rather than to the words themselves? Suppose, instead of scolding the boy, she had said something like the following, *in a supportive, empathic tone:*

> "Stevie, we're not talking about my wrinkles. We're talking about how you act silly in class and how it bothers the other kids. I know it must have upset you to hear that your teacher called me, and that's why you tried to change the subject, but Mommy wants to help you get out of trouble at school."

By essentially ignoring Stevie's provocative remark, she gives it no power. She acknowledges it in a neutral tone but then returns to the subject *she* wants to discuss. Notice, also, that she actually explains to Stevie the meaning behind his own words; she tells him that he brought up her wrinkles in order to change the subject and sidestep the school behavior issue. Once a parent has decoded the meaning behind a child's provocative words or behavior, it's almost always helpful to share that interpretation with the child. Explaining to children the feelings behind their words helps them learn what their most powerful emotions are all about. It also quietly affirms parental authority, making it clear that Mommy and Daddy generally know how to help. Such sharing also helps boys and girls feel safe with their feelings and, at least within certain prescribed boundaries, safe in expressing them.

When parents decode their children's provocative communication, recognize the meaning behind the words, and respond to that meaning rather than to the words themselves, a new kind of interaction becomes possible in which the child, no longer feeling defensive and criticized, becomes ready to engage in real problem-solving with the parent.

## The Kid in All of Us

Think once again about the list of common childhood emotional trials—the one about defeat, disappointment, embarrassment, not getting one's way, and so forth. When grown-ups encounter defeat, disappointment, or embarrassment, they experience many of the same feelings kids do. The only difference is that grown-ups presumably have a little more self-control and are better able to keep their most aggressive impulses in check. Kids deserve our heartfelt empathy as they struggle to adapt to life. They lack the tools for coping that most of us develop with age.

So practice what you preach! If you want your children's provocative communication to stop, you have to stop being provocative yourself. Resist the temptation to respond in kind when a child's language or behavior becomes abusive. Hard as it may be at times, model the kind of behavior you expect from your kids. When you respond to a child's angry remark with an angry remark of your own, he or she hears only the anger, not the meaning behind the words, not the "lesson" you are trying to teach.

"Empathy" is a word you'll encounter again and again in these pages. Kids are inexperienced at coping with all the negative aspects of life. They have limited tools with which to manage their internal emotional responses and their external interactions with others. So parents need to try to practice *empathic* forms of guidance and discipline—guidance and discipline leavened by a humane understanding of children's natural and understandable limitations.

## "I'm Sorry"

"Stay cool and 'empathic' when my kid tells me to shut up?!" you may be thinking. "Don't make me laugh!" Well, nobody said this was going to be easy. Despite the best intentions, almost all parents sometimes "lose it" with their children. They yell back, or even strike back physically.

Not so long ago, the common wisdom was that parents never need feel obliged to apologize to their children. It was as though parent-child relationships were somehow exempt from the standards of behavior we're expected to observe in all the rest of our interactions. But the parent who is big enough and fair-minded enough to apologize to a son or daughter for the lapses in judgment and self-control that inevitably occur usually reaps considerable rewards over time, even if the apologies come a day or more later, after everyone has calmed down. "Nobody's perfect" is a phrase we've all heard again and again. It includes you. When you admit your own imperfection to your child, you're demonstrating a very high form of empathy. You're saying, in effect, "since I'm not perfect, I don't expect you to be perfect either. Nobody's perfect, including me. I just want you to try to be the best person you can be, just as I am trying all the time to be a better person myself."

Consider this example:

Tanya, age eight, is playing with her Legos despite her mother's earlier homework reminder. "Tanya, stop playing and do your homework *right now*!" she exclaims loudly. Tanya throws up her hands in disgust. "You always talk to me so mean, Mom! You are *so mean*!" "Watch your mouth, young lady!" Mom retorts. "If you want more trouble, just keep it up!" "Leave me alone . . ." Tanya mutters as she slouches off to her desk.

Again, the mother responds to the words, not the meaning behind them. Tanya wants to play instead of work. Don't we all? The result of the exchange is simply two angry and now estranged people. How might the situation be "rescued"? As suggested above, the mother's best response at this juncture is an apology. She needs to take responsibility for her part in the unpleasant interaction.

Entering Tanya's room, she says calmly, "I'm sorry I used an unfriendly voice and sounded so mean to you. I know playing is more fun than working. Maybe we need to figure out a better way to talk to each other when you're not ready to do your homework, and I want you to do it right away. Next time, what if I say, 'I know you're having fun playing, but let's get your homework done now so you'll have more time to do whatever you like later'? Would that be better?"

By taking this approach, the mother acknowledges her daughter's feelings and invites her to help devise a solution to the problem. She does not respond to the daughter's declaration that she is a "mean Mommy" with a scolding. She ignores the remark, giving it no power, and returns to her main objective. Then she tosses the ball into Tanya's court, giving her permission to come up with a compromise of her own. She responds to the meaning behind her daughter's words, not the words themselves.

Now . . . does the conversation end there, with Tanya answering sweetly, "Yes, Mommy, when you speak to me like that, I'm always happy to cooperate"? Not likely! In a later chapter outlining specific strategies for change, we'll return to this example and see what further steps this mother must be prepared to take to satisfactorily conclude this episode.

## Charting Your Child's Behavior

Here's a simple exercise that will help shed light on your child's patterns of provocative behavior. Take a piece of paper and make some notes:

◆ How often does your child act provocatively—frequently, once or twice a day, only rarely? Include in your estimate episodes of anger, harsh language, sass, stubborn uncooperativeness, and so forth.

◆ Who is your child most often provocative toward—you, your spouse, siblings, friends, everyone?

◆ Does your child tend to overreact to life's tribulations or exhibit delayed reactions to events, bottling up unhappy feelings? Does he or she project, taking out his or her unhappiness or frustration on parents and siblings when they're not directly involved in the problem?

◆ Now the most important notes of all: What events most frequently precipitate provocative language and behavior in your child? Here are some examples:

  ◆ *Fatigue*—When Billy's tired, he's impossible!

  ◆ *Nervousness*—Jane provokes us when she's tense or anxious, like when we took her to the doctor. On the way there, she argued with everything we said.

  ◆ *Feels ignored*—When I don't pay enough attention to Billy he gets very temperamental and bossy. He says things like, "If you don't play with me right now, you're going to be in big trouble!" Or he's more indirect than that and pesters me about "where I put his Teddy Bear" or how I have to "come here and look at this right now!"

  ◆ *When with peers*—Jane is so well-behaved with us; it's when she's with other children her age that she seems to become short tempered, unwilling to share, and argumentative.

  ◆ *When with brothers and sisters*—Billy just can't seem to get along with any of them. It's a constant battle.

  ◆ *When embarrassed.*

  ◆ *When defeated.*

  ◆ And so on . . .

Look at what you've written. You'll probably find that there are patterns. Kids don't just suddenly say "I hate you." When children are provocative, there's something going on. Does your child behave provocatively mainly when he or she doesn't get his or her way? Do problems occur mostly at bedtime? Do you see any other recurrent scenarios for unpleasant confrontations?

You needn't analyze your findings any more than this for now. The purpose of the exercise is to help you to "stay conscious"—to stay sensitive, *in an ongoing way,* to the meanings behind your child's provocative words. Remember, kids share with adults many of the same desires, needs, fears, and frustrations. They simply lack the experience and tools adults have acquired to manage them. The more knowledge you have of the underlying factors that tend to provoke your child, the more empathically and effectively you can respond. When parents sharpen their sensitivity to the true feelings and motives behind their children's behavior, a new kind of mutual respect becomes possible, as well as a new kind of cooperative interaction that can reduce stress and frustration for everyone.

### Things to Remember About Decoding the Meanings Behind Your Child's Words

- Decoding children's provocative communication means uncovering the meaning behind the words.
- For most children, provocative communication arises from issues like being "left out," embarrassment, hurt feelings, disappointment, defeat, and not getting their way.

(continued)

(continued)

- Before responding to your child's provocation, step back and reflect on the meaning behind the words. Take your time. Leave the room, if need be, to calm down and decide what to do or say next. When you respond in anger, your child hears only the anger, not the lesson you're trying to teach.

- When you feel you understand the meaning behind the words, share that meaning with your child.

- Listen to your own voice. Use a firm, but calm, empathic tone as you respond to the meaning behind the words, not to the words themselves.

- Apologize if your own behavior in any way contributed to the problem.

- Look for ways to problem-solve together with your child. Offer alternatives. Invite participation in finding a solution.

- Children have a strong need to feel understood. Remember the importance of empathy for your inexperienced child's struggle to adapt to life's challenges and frustrations.

- Try to stay conscious of the meanings behind your child's words in an ongoing way.

- Finally, you may find it helpful to read this summary over again and reflect on each of these points. Then spend a day or two just concentrating on putting a couple of them into practice. Wait another day, then tackle another pair of points. Little by little, you'll get better at translating all of these suggestions into one habitual pattern of behavior.

# Decoding the Meaning
# Behind Parents' Words

**W**hen children are provocative, parents tend to respond in a manner even more provocative. Their children's misbehavior gives rise to a host of feelings: anger, confusion, concern, sometimes even painful feelings of rejection. Most of the time, however, I find that parents react provocatively to their children largely out of a sense of helplessness. They don't know how to put a stop to the provocative interaction with their kids, and their uncertainty and frustration pushes them over the edge; they lose their cool—and their tempers.

To alleviate this, I encourage parents to apply to their own behavior the same decoding methods I recommend for their children. It's a two-way street. Mothers and fathers need to understand their own reactions to their children just as clearly as they understand their kids' reactions to them and to the world in general. See if you recognize yourself among the following general "reaction categories":

## Blowing a Gasket

You've told your child again and again to "stop it right this minute!" It doesn't work. You see red. Your nostrils flare. Smoke shoots out of your ears. You grab your kid's arm, squeeze it hard, and make the same demand—this time in a voice loud enough to strip paint. The kid says to himself, "Geez, I guess I'd better stop . . . or else call 911." And he does stop. Until he starts again in an hour, or a day, or a week.

## The Evil Eye

This time the same message is delivered through a form of body language that means, "If you don't stop that this instant, you're going to be sorry!" It's used most often in public or social situations in which a louder or more physical approach might be seen as tacky. The body language consists of lowering the chin, furrowing the eyebrows, and turning the eyes into those laser weapons one sees in video games. This glower, or "look that could kill," is often accompanied by a verbal threat spoken very quietly, through clenched teeth. It's also frequently accompanied by the delusion that no one else has noticed what's going on. The child may respond briefly to the gambit, but usually merely concludes that the parent is a pain in the neck and then resumes the misbehavior.

## The Filibuster

This disciplinary method brings to mind that classic line from the movie *Cool Hand Luke:* "What we have here is a failure to communicate." The parent clings doggedly to the idea that a misbehaving child can be reasoned with, that a long-winded explanation of the logic behind the request to "stop it right now" will somehow result in obedience. Oddly, on rare occasions, this approach actually seems to work. A child will agree with the parent's irrefutable logic and stop causing trouble. But the effect is invariably short-lived, because children's desire to have their own way is stronger than their desire to respond to logic.

## The Raised Hand

Parents who employ this approach believe that sparing the rod will spoil the child. Physical punishments can take many forms, but most involve striking the child with the hand or an object—a hairbrush or some other kind of "paddle." Corporal punishment, while it may seem to be effective in the short term, rarely results in the consistent elimination of provocative behavior, and invariably does real damage. This contention is supported overwhelmingly by numerous research studies. When parents behave aggressively, they are teaching aggression to their kids. They are demonstrating their conviction that, under certain circumstances, it's perfectly okay to inflict physical hurt, even on "loved ones." They are also ruling by fear, and fear fosters rebelliousness, especially a sort of *secret* rebelliousness in which kids feel a deep, internalized resentment of their parents for making them so fearful in the first place. Children who fear their parents cannot fully trust their parents' love for them. The repercussions from this particularly damaging type of uncertainty can last a lifetime.

## Throwing Up the Hands

Translation: "I give up." Many parents reach a point where they simply stop dealing with their kids' provocative communication. They ignore it, they brush it off, or they simply allow their children to "run wild," refusing to intercede no matter how difficult or disruptive their kids become. Such parents may shake their heads in dismay or heave great sighs of resignation, but they do little or nothing to change the status quo, hoping against hope that things will eventually improve if they just "ride it out." Meanwhile, their children conclude, "Mom and Dad are wimps! I can say and do anything I want! No one can stop me!"

## Any or All of the Above

Of course, many parents display more than one of these behavior patterns, depending upon the occasion and their mood. The result for children is confusion. "Exactly what is Mom willing to put up with?" they wonder. Clearly, such disciplinary uncertainty is unproductive.

## Putting Yourself on the Couch

Parents often don't understand or acknowledge the real motivations and feelings behind the things they say and do any better than their children do. It's natural simply to respond directly and instinctively to provocation without taking a moment to ask yourself "What is really upsetting me?" and "What do I really want to say?" If you take a moment to ask yourself those questions—to listen to your own thoughts and feelings and analyze what it is you really want—you will begin to open the door to more effective and satisfying communication with your children. Here are some common feelings behind parents' words. Do any of them apply to you?

## Feeling Rejected

Many parents are extremely sensitive to perceived rejection by their children. The mother who offers her daughter a hug and is pushed away, the father whose son prefers to watch a TV rerun than play a game of catch—both can feel genuinely hurt when such things occur, even though they may recognize intellectually that it's unrealistic to expect constant devotion from their kids. Hypersensitivity to rejection can have roots in a neglectful or abusive upbringing. But most parents experience it now and again regardless of their personal histories. When you feel rejected by your child, does it make you angry? A statement like "How can you say that to me after all I've done for you?!" is accusatory and therefore provocative. As I hope this book will convince you, responding to provocation with more provocation is counterproductive.

## Feeling Guilty

To my mind, there's such a thing as normal, healthy guilt. The parent who loses his or her temper with a child (as almost all of us do sooner or later) and then feels guilty enough about it to try to avoid such lapses in the future is worthy of praise. No one's perfect. So when we behave imperfectly, we should cheerfully admit it to ourselves, think about why it happened, and take steps to minimize the chance of it happening again.

However, some parents habitually behave harshly toward their children and then experience a kind of pervasive guilt and regret afterward—even self-loathing—that causes them to try and "make it up" to their child. This can result in a total loss of appropriate limits on the child's behavior. Meanwhile, such parents sidestep what is really needed under the circumstances: thoughtful examination of the real issues within themselves that caused their harsh behavior in the first place.

## Helplessness

Parents who experience feelings of helplessness in the face of their children's provocative communication generally don't feel very powerful in meeting their kids' emotional needs. This lack of confidence and self-assertiveness causes them to feel overwhelmed, to withdraw from conflict rather than meet it head-on and deal with it decisively. Instead, they either attempt to change the subject or become silent and withdrawn. Such parents can even experience feelings of embarrassment in the face of provocation from their children—

embarrassment over what they perceive as their own weakness and paralysis.

## There Must Be Something Wrong!

Finally, some parents find it inconceivable that their child could be difficult without there being some deeper, more serious problem. Often, they themselves had rather benign, pleasant childhoods, and they can't imagine how their own child can be so much more provocative than they remember being themselves. In the vast majority of cases, their concern is unwarranted, and there is no need for professional intervention. To be sure, some children do need therapy. But far more often, such worries about a child's mental health get in the way of simply becoming more effective as a parent. I hope this book is helpful in that regard, and allays any fears you may have about your recalcitrant child's psychiatric condition.

## Staying Conscious

Throughout this book you'll be encouraged to recognize patterns in your own behavior as well as your child's. When you *stay conscious* of the words you use and the meanings behind them—just as I have urged you to stay conscious of the meanings behind your children's words—you will almost automatically begin to improve your communication skills with your kids. Theirs will start to improve with you, too, because you'll be modeling more effective forms of interaction.

## Things to Remember About Decoding the Meanings Behind Your Own Words

◆ The "meaning behind your words" means the thoughts and feelings that are outside your immediate awareness but that actually direct your behavior and color the things you say. The more aware you become of the inner feelings that affect your interaction with your children, the more constructive your communication will become.

◆ Ask yourself, "How often do I act provocatively with my child?" In other words, make an assessment of how often you meet fire with fire rather than with water!

◆ Listen to yourself. When your child misbehaves, how do you behave? What kinds of things do you say? Write down some examples. It really helps to read back to yourself the words you used when your patience was tested and your child made you angry.

◆ Reflect on what situations provoke you the most. Examples might include "when I'm tired," "when he doesn't follow the rules," or "when we're around other people." What kinds of things do your children say and do that make you most angry? Backtalk? Swearing? Rudeness? Noisiness? Badgering? All of the above?

◆ How often do you "overtalk" to your child? When you go on too long, your child simply tunes out. Limit lectures!

◆ Remember to apologize if and when you react provocatively to your child's behavior. When you have both been provocative, take the lead and say something like, "Both of us didn't behave in a very friendly way toward each other, so I'm sorry for the way I talked to you, and I think you probably feel the same way." If the child does not

(continued)

(continued)

reciprocate with an apology, don't react. Just leave it alone.

◆ After any conflict with your child, take a few moments to reflect on what just happened. At least 80 percent of all the provocative interaction between children and their parents occurs as a result of the immediate situation, and the participants' on-the-spot reactions to it. Ask yourself, "What could I have said differently? How did my own statements and feelings contribute to this conflict?"

◆ When you gain a better understanding of the feelings behind your own words, you will start to find better, more effective words with which to express yourself.

# 5

# Empathic Communication

Empathic communication with children requires parents to share their kids' emotions, thoughts, and feelings; to attempt to see the world, its challenges and mysteries, *through their children's inexperienced eyes without passing judgment or being critical.* When parents become more successful at empathic communication through a deeper recognition and appreciation of their kids' struggles to grow up, the result is invariably a reduction in provocative behavior and a stronger bond between parent and child. Empathic communication is the cornerstone of helping children to feel understood and to be more open to change. The language of empathy is firm but calm. It is simple and direct and never lectures. It is willing to admit fault.

Most parents feel they give their children "unconditional love." But the fact is, most children feel, to one degree or another, that their parents' love does have certain conditions. The parent who subtly, or not so subtly, pressures a child to become a professional like a doctor or lawyer, for example, implies that if the child does not follow that path, he or she will be a disappointment to the parent. Remarks directed at children such as "You're never going to amount to anything if you don't improve your grades" or "You're wasting your potential" can cause a young person to feel that parental love and respect are, indeed, conditional, requiring the attainment of certain levels of achievement. Empathic communication obliges parents to separate what they want for their children from what their children want for themselves, respecting their children for the developing individuals they are and encouraging them to find their own way at their own speed. When parents learn to project a more compassionate understanding of their children's struggles to grow up, actively demonstrating that they comprehend and sympathize with the trials their sons and daughters are going through, conflicts are resolved faster and more lastingly. Indeed, the positive effects of an empathic upbringing linger for a lifetime.

Empathic communication should start at birth. Beyond satisfying their newborn child's basic needs for food and regular diaper changes, most parents quickly learn what seems to soothe as well as stimulate their baby, whether it be singing, smiling warmly, talking "baby talk," or playing with colorful toys. Such nurturing has been shown again and again to have profound effects on infant development, effects that have lifelong implications. As Daniel J. Siegel wrote in his influential book *The Developing Mind*, "The brain's development is an 'experience-dependent' process, in which experience activates certain pathways in the brain, strengthening existing connections and creating new ones."*

---

* Daniel J. Siegel, *The Developing Mind* (New York: The Guilford Press, 1999).

Babies that are actively nurtured and engaged in frequent play and stimulation develop more neural pathways in their brains. They do better in school and in general. When parents are calm and loving, when they engage in empathic communication with their kids as a general rule, their children become more empathic and compassionate themselves. As a result, they tend to prosper personally, socially, and academically.

## Modeling

Kids identify strongly with their parents. This is true even of children who seem to disagree with their mothers and fathers at every turn. Your behavioral style will quickly be absorbed and imitated by your children. So when you interact caringly with your spouse—and even with complete strangers like the plumber or the attendant at the toll bridge—you're giving your children a blueprint for getting along with you, with each other, and with the rest of the world. Conversely, husbands and wives who treat each other critically, impatiently, or disrespectfully—who do not practice empathic communication with each other—shouldn't expect to see much of it from their kids. Sometimes these nonempathic habits are very deep-seated. Parents who were themselves brought up in unempathic ways can find it especially difficult to adopt the practices recommended here. Most of us have read or heard through the media that victims of childhood abuse are the most likely to abuse their own children. This seems counterintuitive. One would think that someone who was mistreated as a child would scrupulously avoid perpetuating the abuse in his own family. But statistically such is not the case. It can be a considerable challenge

to overcome behavioral patterns ingrained since early childhood. Just the same, every display of empathy in the household reaps a reward: the encouragement of empathic habits
in everyone present. And by empathic habits, I simply mean
a willingness to put oneself in another's shoes; to view the
emotions and actions of others with more tolerance and understanding.

## Empathic Home Rituals

Children can be taught empathy. A simple ritual I recommend can be performed nightly at the dinner table. It's especially effective with kids four to seven years of age and
consists simply of spending a few minutes discussing kind
acts that family members have performed in the course of the
day, or intend to perform the following day. Dad might kick
off the ritual one evening by saying, "Kids, we're going to try
something new at dinner, because your mom and I want to
help you learn how to be kind to each other and care about
other people. For just a few minutes each night, we'll all talk
about things we did during the day—at home, or at school, or
at work—that were kind; things we did that helped someone
else. I'll start. Today I kept my promise to Mom to fix the
kitchen faucet." He speaks in a tone that suggests he was
happy to do this for his wife. Mom can then respond, "I was
very glad that Daddy did that. Thank you, honey." Other
family members then follow suit. If a child offers a comment
as simple as "I pet the dog" or "I gave Mommy a kiss," parents
should reply with praise: "That's good, honey! That was a
sweet, kind thing to do!"

When children can't think of anything, don't be critical.

Instead, offer suggestions like "Maybe you could help your sister clean up her room" or ask siblings if they have any ideas to offer. If a child still refuses to participate, simply say, "It's okay if you don't feel ready to do anything, but we really hope you'll think about it because we know you can be really helpful and kind." If and when a child finally participates, but begrudgingly, say something like "You're being very kind to help, but I hope you'll try to do it in a friendlier way next time. It would really be great if you acted like you're happy to help." The point is to encourage empathic behavior *in an empathic way*!

## Empathic Community Rituals

By the same token, parents who extend their empathic behavior into the community by helping their neighbors or by engaging in organized charitable activities further help their children learn to internalize the feelings of others and behave more generously. For example, taking the kids on a regular trip to a local philanthropic organization with a box full of food or outgrown clothing and toys helps them become more aware of the needs of others, as well as of their own comparative good fortune. Parents should encourage their children to help choose the items that will be donated, explaining that the food, clothing, and toys will go to families that can't afford to buy the things they need.

## Empathic Rituals at School

Many schools—both public and private—have a variety of altruistic programs in which children can be encouraged to become involved, from toy and food drives, to tutoring, to teachers' helpers. If your child's school has no such volunteer activities, you might bring up the need at your next PTA meeting. It's not about collecting money, it's about becoming more cognizant of the needs of others and taking it upon oneself to help meet those needs in whatever way one can. It's about teaching children the importance of kindness and generosity, and about experiencing the feelings of satisfaction that charitable acts can generate. Even kids who are them- selves underprivileged can benefit from giving time and as- sistance to those who suffer limitations, whether they be physical, mental, or environmental.

## Recognizing Empathic Acts

Still another powerful tool for encouraging empathic behav- ior in children is to point out examples of kindness as they occur in everyday life:

- ◆ "Honey, did you see how that man took that older woman's arm as she crossed the street? That was very nice of him."
- ◆ "Did you notice how friendly that cashier was at the supermarket? He was so nice to us!"

♦ "Did you see how Daddy helped that little boy who was lost in the store? He was very scared and upset, and Daddy helped him find his mom. Helping other people is very important."

♦ "That was very kind of you to help your brother with his homework."

♦ "Look at this picture in the newspaper of a man rescuing a cat that had climbed into a tree and couldn't get down. He was very nice to do that, wasn't he?"

♦ "Did you notice in your bedtime story that the rooster was very nice to the bunny rabbit? He helped the bunny rabbit find his way home. That was a very nice thing for him to do" or "Did you notice how the friends in the story always tried to help each other? Good friends help each other out."

It's easy to let simple incidents like these pass without comment, but when you call attention to them and point out the little lessons in kindness and empathy they represent, they can become powerful teaching tools. Older kids can be similarly encouraged to take note of acts of kindness. A child who finishes reading a book can be asked, "Did the characters treat each other nicely in the book? Who was nice and who was mean?" It's okay to explain to older kids why you're asking these questions. "I want you to be aware of the importance of how people treat each other," you might say. If the child responds with a comment on who was nice and who wasn't, praise is in order: "That's really observant of you to notice who treated other people kindly and who didn't." Interactions like these don't have an effect overnight, but rather a cumulative benefit over time.

## Empathic "Exercise"

Yet another ritual parents can initiate is one in which each family member in turn creates and carries out an empathic act directed at another family member. At the dinner table, Mom might say, "Kids, we're all going to learn how to be nicer to each other. Each week, one of us will be 'it,' and all of us have to do something especially nice for that person that week. So this first week will be Jimmy Week. Next week will be Jenny Week, and then it'll be Dad Week, and then Mom Week. So during Jimmy Week, maybe you could try not to get mad at Jimmy so much, Jenny. Or you can come up with an idea of your own. That's fine, too. This will help us all be nicer to each other." At dinner each day, a few moments can be devoted to finding out what family members have done to be nice to Jimmy. Remember to praise all efforts and remind everyone of the goal of the exercise—to help everyone learn to be kinder. If a child refuses to participate, don't be critical. Just express the hope that the defector will change his or her mind, and continue to model kind and generous behavior yourself. Most children will eventually fall in line!

### Things to Remember About Empathy

◆ Empathy can be learned.
◆ Children whose capacity for empathy is stimulated and nurtured throughout childhood benefit immeasurably—and so do those around them.

(continued)

(continued)

- To learn empathy, children must experience it from their parents, not just hear about it, or get scolded for the lack of it.
- Empathy helps parents and their kids listen better and hear the meanings behind each other's words.
- Parental empathy helps children feel understood and appreciated.
- Empathic parents are better parents; empathic people are better people, who others like to be around.
- The world needs more empathy!

# Strategies for Change: Incentives and Consequences

Incentives and consequences modify and channel our behavior throughout our lives. Hard work is rewarded with income and job satisfaction. Drive too fast on the interstate, and the consequences can be costly if a state trooper is watching. Since children are motivated primarily by self-interest, incentives and consequences can be powerful behavior modifiers if used wisely and consistently by parents.

## Praise

The simplest incentive you can use to improve your child's behavior is praise. In fact, children who only occasionally behave and speak provocatively can often be "cured" of it completely using "praise therapy" alone.

Parents frequently tend to mete out praise only for major accomplishments, like a goal at soccer practice, an A in math, or a perfectly made bed. To correct provocative behavior, praise must be used much more frequently to reward even small, incremental improvements. For example, if a child makes it through a whole day with less than half the usual provocative outbursts directed at his sister, a parent might exclaim, "You know, you've been much friendlier to your sister today! I'm very proud of you, and I'll bet you can do even better tomorrow!" Don't expect perfection, reserving praise only for a total absence of provocative behavior. Any step in the right direction is worthy of a compliment. When praise is used as part of an improvement process, rather than as a final reward, it becomes a very strong incentive for children. As mentioned earlier, kids have a hard time deferring gratification. Give them praise now, not later, for any step in the right direction!

Preschool children are, of course, very devoted to their parents. Parental praise means a great deal to them, and they show it. Older children may not delight so obviously in praise, but it has a powerful effect on them just the same. Don't conclude that an older child is indifferent to praise just because he or she doesn't beam with pleasure upon receipt of a compliment. Older kids need praise every bit as much as younger ones.

It's also important to be specific about what the praise is for. Don't just say "You've been behaving better today," but rather "You didn't argue when I asked you to clean up your room." Being specific with praise helps children learn exactly what you expect from them and also encourages repetition of the desired behavior.

The ultimate benefit of praise is that it says to your child that he or she is appreciated, that he or she is a source of pride. When parents are proud of their children and let them know it, it helps the children develop pride in themselves.

High self-esteem discourages provocative behavior in general, because children who feel secure have less need to prove their worth and power through aggression.

Finally, when children receive regular praise, they ultimately learn to internalize it, deriving private satisfaction from behaving in ways that have garnered praise from their parents and other caregivers in the past. They experience pleasure and pride in themselves from "doing the right thing," from doing what they have been taught is appropriate and desirable. Thus, after a child has been "cured" of an undesirable behavior pattern, further parental praise becomes unnecessary.

## Just Rewards

Of course, simply praising and encouraging children when they do the right things doesn't always eliminate provocative episodes. Something more is needed. The next incremental step is the tangible reward, tailored thoughtfully to the individual. Tangible rewards have a more powerful effect in reinforcing desirable behavior than praise alone.

Three- to five-year-old children have their ups and downs, and the first question you must ask yourself is whether this reinforcement technique is even needed. Young children can be very provocative one week, then improve considerably the next. It's just the normal, fickle nature of this developmental stage. But if provocative behavior persists in your preschooler, you may want to devise a "progress chart." These charts furnish a way of recognizing improvements in behavior and displaying those improvements for all to see. They also help keep the child's attention on the area of behavior that concerns the parent.

The first step is to construct a simple grid on a piece of paper with lines of boxes labeled with the kinds of behavior that need improvement. Suppose you determined, in the previous chapter's little notebook exercise, that your child is most provocative with his brother when it's time to get dressed and when it's time to take a nap. A progress chart might look something like this:

|  | Mon. | Tues. | Wed. | Thurs. | Fri. | Sat. | Sun. |
|---|---|---|---|---|---|---|---|
| Nice to your brother |  |  |  |  |  |  |  |
| Dressed without argument |  |  |  |  |  |  |  |
| Took nap without argument |  |  |  |  |  |  |  |

Each day, if your child shows improvement in any of the listed areas, you draw a star in the appropriate box (or have your child affix a colorful sticker). Do this at the end of each day for every category. With young children, it's important to make this a daily exercise—preschool kids need prompt reinforcement of desirable behavior.

Every time your child earns a star, be specific about why it's being awarded. Say something like, "James, you were friendly to your little brother all day, so you get a star!" If the child fails to earn a reward, encourage him or her to do better the next day. "Well, you didn't get a star for today's nap because you didn't cooperate when I said it was time to get in bed," you might explain. "But remember, you have another chance to get a star for tomorrow's nap!"

For some kids, a simple star is reward enough; they delight in receiving it. Others may require a more tangible prize—like an inexpensive toy or trinket—before they'll

amend their behavior consistently. These can be kept in a little "grab bag" that the child can reach into at reward time.
Larger prizes can be offered for amassing specific numbers of
stars, like four or five in a row, or a full week's worth. A trip
to the movies or the ice cream parlor is a common choice.
Have the child help keep a tally of the stars as they accumulate, counting the total each day. When the magic number is
reached, it's time for the promised special reward. Small and
large prizes can also take the form of extra stories at bedtime,
a special trip to the park, a favorite food at mealtime, and so
forth.

All rewards, as well as the incremental improvements
required to win them, need to be tailored to the individual,
and it may take some adjusting before you arrive at an effective arrangement. Don't be afraid to experiment, but if you
change a rule, explain why to your child. Say, for example, "I
know this hasn't been easy for you, so this week I'm going to
give you a special prize when you get just three stars instead
of four." Take special care to ensure that any rewards offered
are thoroughly attainable. Particularly with younger children,
if it proves too hard to receive a star, or requires too lengthy
a period to earn a special reward, the incentive will quickly
evaporate and no progress will be made. In fact, it is often
necessary to award a very small or "partial" prize for slight incremental improvements, praising the step forward but explaining that the full prize will be theirs only if they display
the desired behavior *all* day, not for just part of the day. The
bottom line is that it must be nearly impossible for the child
to fail. Incentives only reinforce desired behavior when they
are actually received!

Parents often worry that rewarding good behavior in
this way will make their children expect rewards for everything. The key for three- to five-year-olds is to restrict the

number of entries on the chart to only a few categories. The child will not expect rewards for everything if you refrain from offering them for everything. Work on just two or three issues at a time. When the child shows consistent improvement in one category, you can replace it with another, like "Do it when I tell you" or "Friendly to Mommy all day."

Remember also to remind your child how many stars there are to go before it's time for a special reward. "So far, you have five stars in a row for not fussing at nap time, Janie!" you can say. "Just two more stars, and off we go to the ice cream shop!" Keep that carrot dangling!

The progress chart can work well with six- to eight-year-olds, too, though it's wise to let them choose where to post it. Some kids may feel embarrassed if their friends see it, so you might want to keep it out of sight. And X's or checks may be preferable to stars or stickers for the same reason—they're more "grown-up-looking." Rewards can take the form of extra privileges, like a later bedtime, a sleepover, or anything realistic your child may choose.

Still older children, those in the nine-to-eleven bracket, have typically outgrown the chart approach. With them it's often most effective to strike a deal. "If you can do your homework every night for a week without a fight or even an angry look," you can offer, "we'll go to the new *Robot Bikers from Mars* movie this Saturday." Pick any incentive you know is meaningful, or have your child pick one of his or her own. Unlike preschoolers, for whom parental approval is very important and thus a strong incentive in itself, older kids respond more readily to social incentives—special times with friends, trips to the movies, and so forth. You can also explain to older children that if the incentive program doesn't work, you will move on to consequences: "If rewarding you for talking to us in a friendlier way doesn't work, and you still use a mean tone of voice with us, we'll have to start taking things away from you instead."

Once you have set the parameters for the incentive, do not waver from them. You may choose to give the child a break the first week. For example, if the boy in the example above manages to do his homework without a fight every night but one, you can say, "Because you tried very hard and did your homework without being angry or unfriendly every day but one, I'm going to take you to that movie. But next week you'll need to make it through all five days." The following week, stick to that rule! If your child pesters you for another "break," say empathically, "I know this is hard, but no more second chances." Don't argue with your child about this. Calmly declare the discussion over and walk away. Avoid negotiations!

Regardless of your child's age, try the incentive approach for a month. Within that period, it may be necessary to change the incentive one or more times. If your child appears to tire of or become indifferent to an established incentive, try another one. It doesn't have to be a bigger one, just one that matters to your child. If a variety of meaningful incentives still fails to alter behavior consistently, it may be time to move on to consequences, as described in the next section. Remember to praise your child with each success. Be specific: "You've really been much friendlier to your sister all week. That must make you and your sister feel good, and it makes Mommy and Daddy feel good, too. We're very proud of you!"

Please be reassured that incentives are not bribes. Throughout our lives, we all respond to incentives every day. Without them, there'd be no reason to get up in the morning!

## Weaning from Incentives

Once an incentive program has worked, it can be retired. Simply say to the child, "I'm so proud of you for learning to take your nap without fussing and for being so much friendlier to your little sister! You've done such a good job, we really don't need the chart anymore!" Assess the child's reaction. If he or she really wants to keep the chart, so be it. Continue the program a little longer. If not, take it down. If the child begins to regress after a few days or weeks, reinstate the incentives for another two weeks to a month. If that doesn't work, move on to consequences.

If you have been using a grab bag of little prizes and your child asks whether this treasure trove will cease to exist, say "The prizes were to help you prove to yourself that you can be nicer to your sister and take your nap without arguing. And you've proven it. You can do it! You're getting much better at controlling how you act. We're very, very proud of you!" Such praise may seem like a rather poor substitute for a grab bag of prizes, but most children are delighted with the compliments and accept the loss of the booty—if not immediately, within a few days' time.

## Empathic Consequences

If incentives fail to bring about adequate improvement in provocative behavior, the next step is to put in force a series of escalating consequences. Consequences should not be confused with punishment. They are not designed merely to penalize but to teach self-control. The same might be said of that speeding ticket I mentioned earlier. All of us face consequences for missteps throughout our lives. By "empathic consequences," I mean consequences that are designed to teach and that acknowledge the normal difficulties all children have in managing their more primitive impulses. Empathic consequences are meted out in a supportive tone, not a punitive one. The words and actions you choose as you present your children with consequences must be clear and firm, but moderated by the understanding that all normal children lack the experience and self-control to behave as we would like them to all the time. It's natural for them to require direction and discipline. In fact, some kids really only learn to control provocative behavior when their parents exert steady, assertive power that helps them control themselves, complete with strong consequences for misbehavior. Nonetheless, the key is to maintain an empathic frame of mind no matter how firm the measures may have to be. And don't forget to praise each incremental improvement. Reserving praise only for perfection will slow the process, not speed it up.

Further, by the time a child requires consequences to eliminate provocative behavior, it's likely that the parents have lost their tempers a few times themselves. If your child drives you to the edge of your sanity, withdraw for a little while and try to regain it before resuming any discussion. You may need to apologize to your child, as described earlier. Again, when you respond in anger, your child hears only the anger, not the lesson you are trying to teach. A calm, firm voice is a far more effective tool than an angry shout. When you model the kind of behavior you expect from your child, you and your demands will be perceived as fair. Children have a keen sense of fairness and are quick to resent it if you fail to practice what you preach. They also dislike being wrong. If you admit that you are wrong from time to time, they become more accepting of such shortcomings in themselves and less inclined to respond provocatively when scolded.

So let us imagine that the threshold has been crossed. Your child has failed to respond adequately to incentives and you have decided to put in place a consequence for the next transgression. What should that consequence be? It should certainly be something that matters to your child. A consequence that is too mild will have little or no effect. So it must be something that will make an impression appropriate to the child and to the magnitude of the problem. For some, this might be a bedtime that's a half-hour earlier than usual. For others, it might be a favorite television show denied, a sleepover postponed, or a favorite toy withheld. Almost any consequence can be escalated if need be. For example, a half-hour earlier bedtime can become an hour if required, a one-day loss of a favorite toy can turn into two days, and so forth.

Let's go back to Tanya, the little girl we met in Chapter 3 who wouldn't start her homework. Incentives have failed to work and she's still uncooperative at homework time. Levying consequences right in the middle of an argument tends to fan the flames rather than put them out! So her mother picks a quiet moment the morning after the last unpleasant scene.

"Tanya," she says in a calm, firm voice, "because I love you and think you're such a great kid, I want to help you not get so upset when it's homework time. We keep getting into arguments about when to start homework, and that's no fun for you or for me. So from now on, there's going to be a new rule. From now on, when I first ask you to start your homework, I'll give you ten minutes to begin. If it takes you longer than ten minutes and I have to ask you a second time, you'll have to go to bed one half-hour earlier than usual. I know you like to stay up until your normal bedtime, so I hope you'll make the right choice and follow the new rule." She makes the statement without anger, in an empathic, not threatening, tone. The rule is clear and simple. She also adds the suggestion that it will be her daughter's choice whether to obey the rule or not. That puts the ball squarely in Tanya's court and allows her to remain in control of her own situation, despite the possibility of a consequence for behaving provocatively.

If Tanya obeys the rule, praise is in order. Remember to be specific: "That's great, Tanya! You did your homework right away! I'm very proud of you!" If she fails to improve within two weeks, then the consequence may have to be escalated to an hour. When consequences are applied and managed consistently, most children learn that cooperation is preferable to resistance.

## Consistency and Control

Many parents fail at disciplinary efforts because they adopt a "shotgun approach" to their children's provocative behavior. They wait until the child pushes them over the edge, and then they threaten, shout, and/or deliver a whack to the behind. In the long run, this repetitive and exhausting cycle nearly always fails to alter behavior. If you feel you're too agitated to confront your children in a controlled manner, leave the room and calm down before dealing with the situation. It is only when you're in control that your children will actually listen to you! Surprising as it may seem, there's nothing wrong with dealing with provocative behavior in a quiet moment on the following day. Say to your child, "Remember yesterday when I asked you to clean your room and you said no to me in a very angry way? Well, from now on there's going to be a new rule. If you answer me in an angry way when I ask you to do something, I will ask you *one more time* to change your voice and do what I ask. If you don't, then there will be no video games for a whole day. The next time, there will be no video games for two days. And so on. Do you understand the new rule?"

Here, the parent has clearly and specifically defined an escalating series of consequences in a calm, measured, empathic tone. It doesn't matter that a day has passed since the behavior in question. In this calmer setting, the parent's words will be heard and are far more likely to be heeded.

Needless to say, when rules like these are laid down, the parent must follow through on them *without exception or negotiation*. If the child speaks in an angry tone, remind him or her of the new rule and allow the one promised chance to follow it. If he or she fails, calmly levy the consequence, effective immediately! A rule that is observed only some of the time is almost useless as a behavior modifier. Every deviation from the rule as it was originally defined undermines its effectiveness and delays its results. Be prepared, as well, to escalate the consequence as required, and as you explained to the child. Each time you do so, be sure the child understands the specific reason for the escalation. Explain what is happening calmly and firmly: "Because you spoke to me in an angry tone and didn't cooperate even after I asked you a second time, I'm putting away the video games for the next *two* days, not just one day."

Again, to pick an appropriate consequence, think about what's important to your child. For three- to five-year-olds it may be a favorite toy, which can be withheld for a day. Some parents use time-outs as consequences very successfully. A time-out can be five minutes sitting in a chair or confined to a bedroom. For older children, the most effective consequences tend to be more social in character: a play date denied, participation in a favorite activity canceled. Try a consequence for one to two weeks and see if it works, escalating as needed. Be consistent and unwavering. If there's no improvement, try a different consequence.

Some children will respond after such consequences are employed on just one or two occasions. Similarly, with some children it's possible to use the same consequence over and over. Others quickly become accepting of certain consequences; the penalties quickly "lose their teeth" and have to be changed. Use your judgment. If a consequence doesn't seem to be producing results, change it. Remember, consequences are not punishments. They're tools for teaching children self-control. Kids respond to consequences out of self-interest. When the right consequence has been put in place and is meted out fairly and consistently, it invariably produces improvement.

Finally, guard against creating consequences that are too harsh, like "You're grounded for a month!" or "No birthday party this year!" Such penalties cross the line into cruelty and only foster anger and resentment. Similarly, a consequence like "No bedtime stories for a week" deprives a child of too much loving "snuggle time." *Do not withhold love while enforcing a consequence.* Remember, the purpose of a consequence is to educate, not to let off parental steam or "get back" at a child.

## A United Front

It's vitally important that all caregivers in a household get involved and agree on any and all incentives and consequences and how they'll be administered. That way, the child cannot play one caregiver against another or engage in separate negotiations with Mom, Dad, Grandma, and so forth. This need not be all that difficult. It simply requires a "family meeting" in which the new rules are established and accepted by all. Encourage everyone in the household to read this book!

Divorced parents can face additional complications in establishing a consistent disciplinary style, but the greater the extent to which mothers and fathers who do not live together can adopt similar, empathic modes of interaction with their children, the better it will be for all concerned.

## The Rarely Provocative Child

When your child uses provocative language only occasionally, it's rarely necessary to resort to consequences. Such children tend to be more sensitive in general and have an even greater need for calm from their parents. An angry rebuke can cause them to withdraw; it can even inhibit their emotional growth. So be especially conscious of your tone when you discuss provocative behavior with a usually well-behaved child. And don't be afraid to apologize and start over if you lose your temper.

Let us suppose that Julie, a usually friendly nine-year-old, has just told her mother to shut up—a first for her. Her mother is startled and nearly reacts angrily, but then catches herself and instead responds empathically:

> "Julie," she says calmly, "you must be very, very upset to say that to me. Why are you so unhappy? Please tell me, because I'd like to help." "You always promise you're going to take me to the toy store," says Julie, "but then at the last minute you say no." Mom acknowledges her daughter's feelings. "I understand," she replies, "and I'm sorry I disappointed you. I'll really try to keep my promises better. And I hope you'll remember to talk to me the way you just did instead of saying things like 'shut up.' When you talk to me the way you just did, I can understand what's bothering you better, and then I can try to help."

The mother validated her daughter's feelings, admitted her own responsibility for some of the problem, and refrained from reacting in anger to the words Julie initially chose to express herself. But suppose Julie had been less forthcoming. Suppose she had said she didn't know why she was upset. Again, in an empathic tone, the mother could say, "Well, the next time you're feeling this upset, maybe you can tell me a little sooner that you're in a bad mood and don't know why. Then we can talk about it and I can give you a hug." The key is that the mother's reply is empathic, not angry. A child who feels accepted and understood is far more likely to control provocative urges. It may sound idealized and pie-in-the-sky, but given time and practice, this kind of empathic interaction can and will become the rule, not the exception, in your household.

# The Sometimes Provocative Child

By "sometimes" I mean that there are discernible patterns to the child's provocative behavior, that it is clearly associated with certain situations or relationships. Frequently, children who are only sometimes provocative have not butted heads with their mothers and fathers often enough to find parental will very compelling. Empathic consequences may be required. On the other hand, incentives alone may work if the child is not especially headstrong. You might want to try the latter first, then move on to consequences if necessary. Remember to praise incremental improvements and be consistent in your rule-making and enforcement.

# The Frequently Provocative Child

These children are often members of families that place few or no boundaries on behavior, or in which the parents model provocative styles of communication themselves. Sometimes, too, Mom and Dad have little or nothing to do with it, and the children simply have aggressive, strong-willed personalities. Occasionally, more serious psychological or psychiatric disorders are involved, and we'll discuss those in a later chapter.

The first step is for parents to take an unblinking look at themselves, their disciplinary attitudes, and their personal communication styles. Parents who model aggressive, provocative behavior should not expect anything different from their kids. A loud "Don't you dare say that to me!" teaches your child nothing and merely escalates the conflict. Back off, settle down, confront your child calmly, and project the more empathic style described in these pages.

After you have levied a consequence on your child, remind him or her that a further misstep will bring about an escalated consequence: "Remember, Sally, if you're unfriendly to your brother again tomorrow, you'll have to go to bed a whole hour early, not just a half-hour." This way, you present the child with a choice: either modify your behavior or further penalize yourself. This approach helps to make it clear to the child that consequences are not punishments arbitrarily meted out by a cruel taskmaster. They need not occur at all; it's entirely up to the child—not the parent—to decide whether a consequence will be administered or not.

If the consequence you have chosen for your child involves time-outs of some kind, think in terms of three- to five-minute periods for the three- to five-year-old. Six- to eight-year-olds generally need fifteen-minute increments. Nine- to eleven-year-olds may require thirty-minute consequences before they begin to control themselves. If the behavior persists, then escalate the consequences in additional half-hour increments up to two hours. Older children for whom two hours doesn't prove effective may require full-day "groundings" before they amend their behavior. Such groundings should prohibit all visitors, TV, telephone, and computer use. You can experiment with different lengths of time to see what your child responds to. And don't forget to praise incremental improvements. "You've spoken to me in a much friendlier tone this morning. I can see you're really trying," you might say. "I believe in you, and I believe you can do even better."

Finally, be patient. Things won't change overnight. Give each new approach to your child's provocative behavior, whether incentives or consequences, as much as a month to show significant results. Watch for even small improvements. They mean it's working. If a week or two passes with absolutely no reduction in provocative behavior, escalate the consequences—in general, doubling them is a good rule of thumb. A one-day denial of computer privileges becomes two days, for example. Always make it clear exactly why the consequence is being escalated; also make clear how the child can avoid such escalation the next time. Don't make empty statements like "If I have to tell you one more time, you're going to be in trouble!" Instead, spell out exactly what you're displeased with: "If you say mean, hurtful things like 'shut up' or 'I hate you' again, you will not go to baseball practice this week. I know you like baseball practice. I hope you'll control yourself so you don't have to stay home."

Above all, the empathic parent remembers that provocative behavior is a normal part of a child's struggle to grow up. Empathic parenting means accepting this struggle and openly sympathizing with it, even while applying firm discipline. It is only in this empathic context that adults and their children can begin to problem-solve together.

## What Is Problem-Solving?

Problem-solving is a process by which parents teach their children how to use their thinking and feeling skills to deal with conflict. The earlier children are introduced to problem-solving techniques, the better. When problem-solving is a household's standard practice, children tend to behave less provocatively in general because they are not exposed to the standard vocabulary of conflict—angry voices, threats, and so forth.

Too often, parents respond to their children's provocative behavior with lectures or lost tempers. They demand obedience, period—usually with raised voices. But such responses are missed opportunities to help kids advance their social and emotional development. When mothers and fathers make a habit of communicating with their children empathically, the children, in turn, become more empathic. This not only reduces conflict in general, it also diminishes the intensity of conflict when it does occur. I have described incentives and consequences as learning tools rather than punishments. Indeed, their basic function is to help children learn how to problem-solve. Kids aren't born with this ability hard-wired into their brains. They need adult help as they struggle to deal with the complexities of life and their relationships with the people around them. Indeed, many adults aren't very good at problem-solving either, and need to learn almost as much about it as their children do!

In a nutshell, problem-solving means taking the time to help children arrive at a resolution and, if need be, employing incentives and consequences to support that resolution. The earlier in a child's life you practice this approach, the better that child will deal with conflict as he or she gets older.

Imagine several kids playing in the backyard. An argument begins over a toy and who's next in line to play with it. Stepping in to referee, a problem-solving parent calmly offers the children opportunities to explain their respective sides of the issue. Next, the parent asks, "Who has an idea on how we can solve this problem?" If one child offers a solution, the parent asks the others for reactions. If a meeting of the minds is reached, praise is in order for solving the problem in a friendly way. If not, the parent offers a choice: "I'll give you all five minutes to come up with a solution to the problem. If you can't, I'll suggest a solution myself. If you reject my solution, then you'll have to stop playing altogether until you find a solution you're happy with." The suggested solution can be as simple as a coin toss. However the conflict is ultimately resolved, this problem-solving approach is far more instructive and satisfying for all concerned than the standard barked order from the grown-up. And the greater effort is worthwhile because of the overall reduction in conflict that invariably results the more these problem-solving techniques are put into practice.

## Things to Remember About Incentives and Consequences

◆ The simplest incentive is praise. Use it frequently, even for small, incremental improvements in behavior. Be specific: Tell your child exactly what the praise is for.

◆ When an undesirable behavior pattern has been corrected, frequent praise ceases to be necessary; the child has internalized it, deriving personal satisfaction from "doing the right thing."

◆ Progress charts can be very effective with younger children, up to about age eight. They can be tied to a variety of rewards, from extra bedtime stories to prizes from a grab bag.

◆ Try incentives for a month, changing them as needed. If you don't get results, move on to consequences.

◆ Empathic consequences are not punishments. They teach children appropriate limits, and they are administered calmly and firmly, never in anger. If you're too upset to levy a consequence in a calm tone, wait until you can.

(continued)

(continued)

- Devise consequences that can be escalated in simple, logical ways if and when the need arises.
- Once a set of consequences has been defined, follow through on them consistently and without negotiation. All family members need to be involved and "on the same page."
- If a consequence seems to be losing its "teeth," change it.
- Every child is different. Rarely, sometimes, and frequently provocative kids require different responses from their parents.
- Be patient. Then, be *more* patient!
- Problem-solving is the goal. It is the new kind of behavior that will take the place of angry conflict if the techniques I describe in this book are applied effectively.

# Your Child's Personal Style and Temperament

When children misbehave, their moms and dads may ask themselves, "What have I done wrong?! How have I failed as a parent?! Have I created a monster?!" To be sure, parents must be willing to analyze their own behavior—and that means not only their behavior toward their children but their behavior toward others *in the presence of* their children. Just the same, kids' provocative behavior often arises not just from nurture but nature as well. "Temperament" is defined as the general manner of thinking, behaving, and reacting characteristic of a specific individual. Most experts agree that children's inborn genetic makeup is responsible for about 50 percent of their temperament. So whether your child is as stubborn as a mule or as amenable as a puppy may have as much to do with genes as upbringing.

Does this mean that parental attempts to correct provocative behavior are doomed to failure virtually half the time? Can one pick a fight with Mother Nature and win? Of course. Daniel J. Siegel's remarkable book *The Developing Mind*, which I quoted earlier, also states, "The question isn't 'Is it heredity *or* experience?,' but 'How do heredity *and* experience interact in the development of an individual?' "* The fact that your child may be genetically predisposed to fits of anger or uncooperativeness doesn't mean there's nothing you can do about it. Most of us have taken steps to adjust quirks in our own personalities, and there's no reason why children with predispositions toward provocative behavior can't be taught self-control. In other words, caregivers can help children experience ways of behaving that ultimately counteract undesirable inherited traits.

Let's look at some of the basic categories of temperament and see how they relate to provocative behavior. Of course, all children exhibit a wide variety of behaviors and emotions. But when a particular kind of behavior or emotion is displayed consistently and really seems to "come out of nowhere," it may represent something that's part of the child's natural makeup. "He's been this way since he was an infant" is a remark I often hear from parents. If you're convinced it's part of your child's fundamental nature to be difficult, don't despair. The tools I describe in this book will still work!

Finally, the categories below are generalizations, and every child is different. It's unlikely you'll find a perfect description of your son or daughter. My hope is that by describing some common personality types, you'll gain more insight into what's going on in your own child's head, whichever combination of these traits he or she may display. As you know by now, "empathy" is a favorite word of mine. The better you understand how your developing child's mind works,

---

* Daniel J. Siegel, *The Developing Mind* (New York: The Guilford Press, 1999).

the better and more intuitively you'll be able to apply the remedies taught here.

## Hair Trigger—the Reactive Child

As the name implies, these kids react strongly to life. On the bright side, reactive children are usually energetic, enthusiastic, and verbal. They can be quite empathic and sweet. When they're happy, they let you know it, laughing delightedly and openly expressing affection. By the same token, reactive children object vociferously when things don't go their way. Right from the cradle, they tend to scream, not merely cry, when they're unhappy. Reactive toddlers are impatient and tantrum-prone. At preschool age, they may stamp angrily out of the room when they don't get their way. Typical remarks include "No!" "You can't make me!" "I don't want to!" "Go away!" "You cheat!" and "Leave me alone!" They're often rather poor losers and have difficulty apologizing or admitting they're wrong. They're quite unafraid of authority, would rather make their own rules, and seem unconcerned about upsetting their parents.

The bottom line is that reactive children, whether from nature or nurture, haven't learned to express negative feelings in any way other than impatient, angry outbursts. Even when they're sad, insecure, or fearful, the result is often provocative communication rather than more appropriate responses like fretfulness or outright tears. Reactive children don't like to feel emotionally vulnerable, and as a result, they can be hard to comfort. Usually, with time, they develop a more varied and appropriate set of responses to life's ups and downs. But until they do, they can be quite a handful!

Parents need to help reactive children control their outbursts by setting firm but empathic limits and applying the incentives and consequences described earlier as required.

Remember, too, that when mothers, fathers, and siblings respond to a reactive child's outbursts with outbursts of their own, the behavior is only perpetuated. Don't model the very thing that's driving you crazy! To teach self-control, you must first control yourself.

## The Moody Child

Reactive kids have no difficulty expressing what's bothering them. Moody children are quite the opposite. They keep their thoughts and feelings to themselves. Sometimes peers and parents alike interpret this as unfriendliness or outright hostility. But interestingly, most moody children do not describe themselves as unhappy. They typically function pretty well and can be quite cooperative most of the time.

Moodiness generally doesn't become evident until preschool age. Then parents may begin to worry that their son or daughter seems sad much of the time. In fact, moody children simply have difficulty expressing feelings openly. They internalize them. Their reticence is easy to interpret as unhappiness, even when they're feeling quite content. Nonetheless, moody children generally do not feel particularly powerful. They may not ask for help when they encounter difficulties. They frequently play alone, and their social skills may be slow to develop. Moody children are often somewhat uncomfortable with themselves, though they may not be fully aware of it or able to discuss it. Provocative outbursts often betray a suspicion or belief that the world is against them, a "poor me" perspective on life. Typical remarks may include "Stop picking on me!" "Everybody hates me!" or "I never do anything right!" Moody children also make statements that distance them from other family members and from peers: "Leave me alone!" "Stay out of my room!" "I don't want to talk to you!" "Stop bothering me!"

Parents need to understand that moody children can't be cajoled into a brighter outlook with cheerful remarks. Modeling gaiety won't induce it in the child. Instead, it's best to take the child's apparent feelings seriously and encourage as much communication as possible. Be an active listener and encourage the moody child to talk things out aloud with you.

For example, open a discussion with a remark like: "Honey, I could see that you were in a very bad mood after learning that Hannah couldn't come over to play with you. Am I right?" If the child nods or acknowledges this in any way, praise the response: "It's really good when you tell me what upsets you. I understand how very disappointed you were that Hannah couldn't come over." This validates the child's feelings and shows that you sympathize. If the child says even more, praise it specifically. Say "You really know how to tell me what's bothering you. That's great. It lets me help you, and I really like to do that." If the child doesn't verbalize at all, accept the silence and encourage better communication next time: "It's okay if you don't want to tell me now. Maybe you can tell me later." Ask the question again after some time has passed—perhaps the next day. You may even need to employ an incentive to encourage a reply, for example: "If you'll talk with me a little about how you feel, we'll have an extra story tonight. Think about it, and I'll ask you again a little later." The key is to be calm and patient. With time, moody children can be coaxed out of their shells.

Finally, if your child is frequently withdrawn and persistently exhibits dark moods, it may be advisable to consult with a psychotherapist, who will be better able to differentiate between moodiness and more serious depression.

## Pleeeeease?!—the Persistent Child

Almost all children can be very persistent at times. "Mommy, please? C'mon, Mommy! Can't I? Pleeeaaase??? Mommyyyyyyyy?!" Every parent has heard it. But when a child is persistent—or should we say *insistent*—over a great many issues, week in and week out, it may be part of his or her basic temperament. In fact, the persistent temperament may even begin to show in infancy with prolonged, impatient crying. Persistent children are often successful, assertive, full of energy and life, and fun to be with. But when they go on a rampage for something they want—or feel that a parent, sibling, or peer isn't being fair to them—watch out!

Persistent children haven't learned to delay gratification. They can be downright obsessive about getting their needs met, refusing to stop pestering their parents or siblings even when threatened with rather dire consequences. Provocative behavior often takes the form of whining, as opposed to belligerence. Persistent children usually don't understand how annoying their behavior can become. When ignored or punished, they can feel grievously wronged and misunderstood. Such frustration only serves to perpetuate the persistent behavior pattern and can also foster a state of general anxiety. Sometimes, when ignored or denied what they want, persistent children will issue threats like "If you don't do $x$ for me, then I won't do $y$ for you!" This provocative pattern only makes matters worse, of course, and the situation deteriorates further.

Like the reactive children described earlier, persistent children need strong boundaries enforced by incentives and consequences. They would rather continue to argue than surrender and not get their way. So parents must be prepared to draw the line and employ all the tools described in these pages.

## Handle with Care—the Sensitive Child

These children can be comparatively easy to raise because they're not very assertive or demanding. But to some parents, they can often *feel* provocative because they react "overemotionally." The sensitive infant is upset by loud noises and unfamiliar faces, dislikes change, and cries easily. Older sensitive kids are upset by teasing or scoldings. They lack resilience and "take things hard." For this reason, they can have difficulty with some of their peers, who may characterize them as babies. Sensitive children may do well academically, but underneath it all they don't feel very powerful. They lack assertiveness and have difficulty standing up for themselves. This tendency can persist into adulthood, accompanied by a general lack of self-esteem.

Parents need to remember first that sensitive children can't help the way they are. It may be their fundamental nature, and they may not fully understand or be able to control it at their young age. Strong parents sometimes feel real disappointment in their sensitive children. Boys, especially, are admonished by such parents for being "crybabies," or they're pushed into competitive sports prematurely, making them feel even less powerful when they're unable to hold their own.

Sensitive children need help in learning to express themselves more openly, in making their feelings known more assertively. Encourage them to talk about their fears and other sources of upset, and when they do, encourage them further: "I can understand how that upset you, and I'm really glad you let me know about it!" Little by little, sensitive children can be helped to become more resilient. It just takes time, and above all, empathy.

## Busy Bee—the Active Child

The beginnings of this behavior are visible in early childhood. These are the kids with "ants in their pants." You don't take *them* for walks; they take *you* for walks, tugging at you impatiently. Parents and teachers sometimes wonder if these highly active kids have attention deficit disorder.* More often than not, they don't. They just like being on the go.

When they don't pay attention to requests, it's usually not because they're being contrary; it's because they're too busy enjoying themselves. They ricochet from one activity to the next, provoking parents and siblings not so much by what they verbalize as by what they do—deserting their parents in public places, running down the aisles of stores, and leaving a trail of disarray behind them. They prefer outdoor activities to indoor ones, have trouble sitting still for long periods in school, dislike cleaning up after themselves, and never seem to require "down time." Most often, they're boys, but there are plenty of very active girls, too. It's at its worst in the first five years, after which it usually subsides . . . albeit slowly. In the meantime, parents can feel quite overwhelmed.

On the bright side, active kids are full of life and keen enthusiasms. They can derive great pleasure from afterschool physical pursuits like karate and soccer, and parents should try to enroll them in such activities while also encour-

---

* Kids with true ADD squirm excessively and often fidget constantly with their hands. They are very easily distracted, have difficulty waiting their turn, blurt out answers disruptively before being called on, and have great difficulty following instructions. They also have trouble playing quietly and often intrude on others' activities. Most of the active children I have worked with show few or none of these characteristics.

aging them, using the methods described in these pages, to control themselves when appropriate. As they settle down with age, slowly learning to manage their frenetic tempera- ments, they can be a real delight to raise, channeling their energies into leadership positions in school and constructive extracurricular involvements. Active kids aren't so much op- positional as they are simply delighted to be alive.

Parents should make it a practice to tell active chil- dren what is expected of them ahead of time. Be specific. For example, before arriving at the supermarket, say something like, "Jonathan, while we're shopping, I want you to stay near me so I can always see you. Remember, if you can see me, I can see you. If you run away and don't stay where I can see you, there will be no play date this afternoon." Use the incentives and consequences I've described to help highly ac- tive children learn structure and self-control.

## The Worried Child

Worried children are often very kind and sensitive to the needs of others. They're generally well-liked by their peers, and outside of their worries, they function well. Frequently, one or both of their parents display a similar "worried" dispo- sition. Whether the child's behavior in such cases is imitative or genetic, or both, can be hard to tell. But parental overpro- tectiveness can certainly give rise to a general state of anxiety. In particular, parents who are in the habit of spelling out worst-case scenarios for their kids run the risk of turning them into worriers. By this I mean parents who frequently say things like "Be careful, Johnny! You could fall and break your arm!" It's better to make such remarks only when a real and imminent threat is present.

Worried children have strong separation anxieties, are overconcerned about getting hurt, and adapt poorly to change.

They may become very upset if their parents argue, concluding that a divorce is imminent. Some ask frequent questions about fears they harbor of kidnapping, burglars, monsters, and the like. They may pepper departing parents with questions about where they're going, when they'll be back, why they have to go at all, and so on. In essence, worried children habitually imagine the worst thing that can happen rather than the best thing. For them, the glass is half empty, not half full.

To many parents and siblings, the intense worry becomes a form of provocation. Other family members become impatient with the child's tendency to catastrophize everything, and harsh words are the result. In other instances, parents become concerned that there's something seriously wrong with the child, that he or she is suffering from depression. The parents' worry, communicated in subtle verbal and nonverbal ways, only exacerbates the problem. In the vast majority of cases, the tendency to worry too much abates as the child grows older and gains more experience with life. Parents can help by calmly reassuring the child and explaining why certain of their worries are unwarranted. It's not enough to say, "Oh, don't worry about that, Sally!" or "It's silly to worry about that!" Sally needs to hear exactly *why* her worries are inappropriate. Often, such children need to be reassured again and again.

You can also sometimes help by changing the subject and explaining why in a very focused way. Say, "Sally, you're having trouble being strong inside right now, so we're going to stop talking about this and do something else. What would you like to do? Shall we play a game or go outside? You decide, and I'll go with you." Getting out of the worried frame of mind in this way is often enough to put the matter to rest for a while, and the more time the child spends not worrying, the more that frame of mind will become the dominant habit.

In general, allaying children's fears requires considerable care and creativity. A child who is afraid of mice can benefit from a visit to a pet store, for example. Similarly, a child who is afraid of the dark might be given a flashlight or allowed to sleep with more than a tiny nightlight on. Ask worried children what they think might help them; problem-solve with them. Often, they can engineer an improvement themselves.

## The Preoccupied Child

Children with a preoccupied temperament are usually easygoing, friendly, and nonaggressive. They're just in their own worlds much of the time. They enjoy imaginative play, entertaining themselves alone for long periods. As they grow older, they favor immersive, role-playing video games. So, in general, they require less parental attention and direction. Problems can arise, however, because of what might be called "passive resistance." Preoccupied children may be very slow to respond to requests, and indeed, may not even hear them until they're repeated—loudly! Frequently, preoccupied children are genuinely perplexed when their parents or siblings express frustration and anger over jobs left undone or requests unfulfilled. They often fail to hear what is asked of them, even though they may nod in apparent agreement and mumble "okay" or "uh-huh." It's as though they're only about one-third present. The rest of them is still trying to slay that computer-screen dragon. Meanwhile, Mom and Dad are about to scream!

What to do? Remember that the preoccupied child is typically agreeable and compliant at the bottom of it all. He or she needs consistent, specific follow-through from parents whenever they make a request. An admonition like "James, go to your room and get your coat; we're leaving soon" sounds specific, but it doesn't go nearly far enough. Spell it all out. In a kind but firm voice, say something like "James, go to your room right now and get your coat. Don't stop along the way. Don't do anything else in your room. Just pick up your coat and come straight back here." In some cases, parents may have to check on the child after a couple of minutes to see that the directions are being followed. Consequences may have to be employed if there's no improvement within a couple of weeks: "If I have to come to your room and get you, there will be no computer games when we get back." In particular, mothers and fathers should be careful about the words they use to express their frustration with or disapproval of "spacey" behavior. I remember one family that took to referring to their very bright but preoccupied boy as a "lovable dimwit." Such remarks can do real damage, even when they're supposed to be "just kidding."

## Parents' Personal Styles and Temperaments

Did you think I was going to let you Moms and Dads off the hook? As mentioned, parents' personal temperaments—their ingrained tendencies to behave and react in certain ways—can have profound effects on their children's emerging temperaments. We were all kids once, so, as might be expected, parents' temperaments tend to fall into the same broad categories we've already discussed. That's not to say that parents necessarily share their children's temperaments. They can be as different as night and day. Further, mothers' and fathers' behavior patterns can be greatly affected by their kids' behavior. A provocative child can "bring out the worst" in parents and siblings. Even the most mild-mannered parents can "lose it" when a son or daughter pushes their buttons too persistently. Let's take a look at how parents' temperaments can interact with their children's.

## The Reactive Parent

When the chips are down, these are outgoing, sociable people. When they're happy, they show it, but there's no mistaking when they're unhappy either. In fact, they tend to react poorly to stress and can become angry, aggressive, and overpowering, particularly with similarly reactive or persistent kids. Sensitive or worried children typically become fearful of such parents, surmising that all hell will break loose if they make a misstep. Moody or preoccupied children may distrust reactive parents and feel "unsafe" expressing their feelings to them, even though their relationships are peaceful most of the time. By following the steps outlined in this book and adopting a more empathic attitude toward their children's provocative communication, reactive parents can increase their awareness of their own behavioral excesses and start to curb them. Being less reactive gives less power to whatever you're reacting to. As we've discussed, children are very self-involved; they want attention. When you react passionately to provocation, you are, in fact, delivering something your child wants. When you cease to deliver such strong reactions, you reduce your child's temptation to provoke you in the first place.

## The Moody Parent

Moody parents often are not particularly aware of their moodiness. But they tend to withdraw from their children—and everyone else for that matter—when they're in a bad mood. In such cases, children can fear that they are somehow responsible, that they are the cause of the apparent pain or hostility. This gives rise to guilt, which may come out in a variety of ways, from similar withdrawal to a panoply of later problems. Moody parents are less likely to engage and argue with reactive and persistent children. Instead, they feel overwhelmed or even hurt. Sensitive or worried children may receive empathy from these parents when they're in the right mood to tune in and respond. If they're not, they fail to offer much support. Moody parents have the most difficulty with very active or preoccupied children, because such boys and girls require a lot of emotional energy from their caregivers. The moody parent has a hard time maintaining that consistent emotional focus all day long, and the result can be impatience and pent-up anger.

The best course for such parents is simply to tell their children when they're not in the right mood to interact. In a caring tone, say something like, "Rebecca, Mommy doesn't feel like talking about that right now. But I will discuss it with you tonight before bed." Then be sure to follow through on your promise. Be specific about when you'll be available to your child. If you fail to keep your promise, apologize. Admit that it was your fault, not your child's, and set another time. Similarly, apologize if your mood causes you to overreact to your child and lose your temper. If you recognize that you were at fault, even partly, it's appropriate and constructive to say you're sorry before proceeding with any further attempts at problem-solving.

## The Persistent Parent

Persistent parents can be very patient, understanding, and supportive. By the same token, they can feel very dissatisfied until problems are completely solved and lessons are completely learned. This obsessive streak leads them to lecture provocative children, admonishing them in too much redundant detail. Reactive and persistent kids may argue right back, and confrontations are thereby prolonged. On the other hand, sensitive or moody children can be driven to tears by excessive lecturing, while active or preoccupied children simply go about their business and tune out the parent altogether. In every case, the result is counterproductive, and overpersistent parents need to recognize the tendency within themselves and try to curb it. Limit admonitions to two on any specific subject. If this isn't enough, proceed directly to the incentive and consequence strategies already discussed. This isn't easy, because persistent parents' intense focus on the situation at hand often leaves them oblivious to the negative effects their behavior is having on others.

Here's a helpful exercise: If you feel you might be an overpersistent parent, make a pact with yourself to defer responding to your child's provocation for an entire morning or afternoon. As provocations occur, note them and their cause on a slip of paper. Later, look at the list and reflect upon what happened as a result of your inaction. It's likely that the world continued to spin on its axis, unperturbed. So try to lighten up. Many of the conflicts between parents and kids aren't really all that serious. Excessive persistence nearly always does more harm than good.

## The Sensitive Parent

Sensitive parents tend to be kind and gentle. They have little difficulty feeling empathy for provocative children. Sensitive parents are highly motivated to get to the bottom of their kids' feelings and then share that knowledge with them so they can learn from it. But they can also be genuinely hurt by things their children say to them, taking provocative or aggressive remarks very personally. Worse still, these parents often have a lot of trouble setting strong boundaries when provocative behavior gets out of hand. It's simply against their nature to put their feet down and be strict and unrelenting, even when the situation clearly requires that limits be set and maintained. They're too easily swayed by the reactive or persistent child's pleadings, and they're likely to harbor guilty fears that they're being too hard on the moody, sensitive, or worried child. The active or preoccupied child's inattentive behavior often fails to irritate them; they don't see it as provocative, and so do nothing about it, even when it really needs attention.

Sometimes it makes sense for the sensitive parent to defer to a less-sensitive partner when it comes to laying down the law. The sensitive mother might ask the father—or a grandparent or other close caregiver—to establish incentives and consequences when they're required, and to be the primary "enforcer." Another approach for the sensitive parent is to practice being firmer about minor disciplinary matters, to help "build the muscle" before tackling more serious problems. For example, when a child asks for a second toy after just having been bought a new one, the parent can say, "No, I'm sorry; one toy is all we're buying today." Then don't back down! By increments, sensitive parents can dispel inappropriate feelings of guilt associated with saying no to their children.

## The Active Parent

Busy-as-a-bee adults usually enjoy their world. They tend to be positive and interactive, frequently involving their kids in family activities. They think rather highly of themselves and model good self-esteem for their children. If they have any problem with provocative communication from their kids, it's usually a lack of patience. Busy-busy people have no time for "nonsense"; their schedule is too full to leave any room for argument or unpleasantness. Active parents are often less reactive to provocation for the same reason. They have a higher "threshold" and are less likely to personalize aggressive talk from their kids; less likely to feel, much less hold on to, emotional hurt. But when provocative behavior goes too far—even for them—they profit as much as anyone from employing the tools I've outlined.

Active parents and their kids benefit from consciously slowing down on a regular basis and having one-on-one "quiet times" together. These interludes can take the form of leisurely walks, story readings, or even just relaxed talks on park benches. Constant activity is fun and exciting, but serenity is good, too. It encourages truly listening to one another, something that can get lost when schedules are packed too tight. Active parents sometimes simply miss great opportunities to communicate with their kids. Because they have other, more important fish to fry, they may fail to follow through on promises, or to notice when their children have pressing needs. By the time they're finally ready to connect with their kids, too much time may have passed. Remember, to children, a half-hour can seem like an eternity. Kids need to feel that they've been heard, that their needs are acknowledged when expressed, not pushed aside by a constant whirl of activity.

## The Worried Parent

On the positive side, worried parents focus a lot of attention on their children. They're emotionally sensitive to their kids' feelings and needs and offer plenty of support when it's needed. But worried parents also tend to be overprotective because they habitually fear the worst. They give warnings like "Don't climb on that, Billy! You might fall and break your bones!" This is not to say that children never need to be cautioned when there is a slight possibility of serious injury. But constant dire warnings can produce an overly concerned child whose natural and healthy sense of adventure has been squashed.

Active, reactive, persistent, and preoccupied kids all tend to ignore worried parents' warnings. "I won't get hurt, Mommy," they sing out, utterly unconcerned—or they don't respond at all. Moody, sensitive kids, on the other hand, may quickly come to believe that the parent is right and they should stay on the sidelines. They can become overly concerned about dangers both real and imagined. The problem is compounded, of course, with the worried child. Frequent dire warnings from worried parents can cause children of the same temperament to harbor serious fears. The child's resulting withdrawal and often very obvious distress only serves to worry the parent more, and the situation worsens. Worried parents have to work very hard to manage their excessive concerns and refrain from projecting them onto the children they love. Better simply to say "Look both ways before crossing the street" than "Look both ways before crossing the street, or you'll get hit by a car and killed!" Caution is wise and desirable; constant apprehension is not.

## The Preoccupied Parent

The preoccupied child usually has at least one preoccupied parent. And preoccupied parents were probably preoccupied children themselves at one time! Self-absorbed mothers and fathers whose heads are "in the clouds" are by no means ineffective parents; their behavior can help foster independence in their children. Preoccupied parents tend to tune in to their children only when something is wrong. If everything seems to be going fine, their minds are elsewhere. This tendency can make them insensitive to the more subtle signs that a child needs help, or empathy, or just simple attention. Kids need to feel that their parents are available to them emotionally.

Further, children need to learn about structure and focus from their caregivers. Often, preoccupied parents find it difficult to create structure and focus because they lack it themselves.

It's very difficult for preoccupied parents to change. Their heads will probably remain in the clouds much of the time, even when they're aware that it causes problems. A more realistic solution for such parents is literally to set regular "appointments" with their children—a daily fifteen minutes or half-hour, perhaps after school or before bedtime—when they sit down with their kids, interact with them in as focused a way as possible, and bring up any issues that need discussion. A brief daily ritual like this can have a profound effect on a child's perception of his parents' availability. It can also help a child who has become too preoccupied himself to learn to connect with others.

## Things to Remember About Temperament

- ◆ Grown-ups need to assess and sometimes take steps to adjust their own temperaments before they can hope to adjust their kids' temperaments.
- ◆ Parents' own ingrained behavior patterns can be just as provocative as their children's.
- ◆ Most experts agree that temperament is about 50 percent nurture and 50 percent nature.

(continued)

(continued)

- ◆ Regardless of whether a personality trait is the result of nature or nurture, it can be changed using the tools described in this book.
- ◆ The categories of temperament described in this chapter are generalized, and individuals are unique. Your child—and you yourself—probably have traits from more than one of the categories. But I hope the way I have discussed temperament helps you to understand and empathize with your child's behavior patterns, as well as to recognize behavior patterns in yourself.
- ◆ Clashes of temperament occur not just when parents and their children have different personality traits, but when they have very similar ones, too.

# Provocative Communication
# Line by Line

Now let's move from the general to the specific. We've discussed in rather broad terms the different categories of provocative communication and the important role it plays in your child's development. We've talked about decoding and responding to the meaning behind the words rather than to the words themselves, and about setting boundaries on behavior through incentives and consequences. We've also examined the issue of temperament—your child's and your own. But how can all this knowledge be applied in real-life situations?

This chapter consists of a series of specific scenarios—scenarios that occur in one form or another in millions of households every day. In each case I'll describe what typically happens, and then what I believe should happen if your child's provocative communication is to be brought under control. Of course, I can't possibly outline every scenario that can occur, though I include scenes between parents and children who are rarely, sometimes, and frequently provocative. You'll have to "mix and match," looking for incidents and interactions that sound familiar to you. Even when I describe a situation or behavior that never occurs in your family, I believe you can benefit from reading the suggested responses. The purpose of all this is to help you acquire a new vocabulary for interacting with your child, an empathic vocabulary built around a new understanding of, and appreciation for, your child's developmental level and emotional needs. Don't expect results overnight. It takes practice, and then more practice. But given time and the consistent application of these principles, your child's behavior will improve markedly.

## Heather's Sleepover

Heather, age nine, is rarely provocative. But one Friday afternoon after school, she asks her mom if her friend Mary can stay for the night. Mom is feeling a bit frazzled. "No, Heather," she replies. "Not tonight." Heather begins to whine and plead. "Heather, I said no," Mom repeats. "You're so *mean*!" Heather exclaims hotly, stamping her foot. Mom, now thoroughly exasperated, points her finger at her daughter and scolds, "You keep this up, young lady, and you'll never have a sleepover again!" Heather exits angrily, fighting tears.

Now imagine an altered scenario. Heather becomes angry, just as above, but Mom takes a deep breath and addresses her firmly, but empathically. "Heather," she says, "I can see you're very upset that Mary can't sleep over tonight. You usually don't act this angry, so I know you're very disappointed. Try to get control of yourself, and then we'll plan a night very soon when Mary can come over."

If Heather responds even slightly more cooperatively, Mom says, "I really appreciate how you're controlling yourself. Let's figure out two good times that Mary can stay the night. Then we can call her and see which one is best for her." If Heather agrees, then Mom adds, in a neutral tone, "Maybe next time I have to say no to you, you can use a friendlier voice and say, 'Can we talk about this and figure out how to solve the problem?'"

Sounds pie-in-the-sky, doesn't it? Remember, in this example, Heather is a rarely provocative child, which improves the chances for a rapid resolution like the one described. The primary lesson here is that the mother responds to the meaning behind Heather's words, not to the words themselves. She remains calm. She does not display anger and, instead, models the kind of behavior she wants from her daughter. By ignoring Heather's provocative reaction, she gives it no power. She empathically acknowledges Heather's disappointment, reminding her that she rarely gets so angry. Then she suggests a way to solve the problem, alleviating the immediate disappointment and suggesting a different way of acting in the future.

## Noisy Jimmy

This six-year-old has a habit of racing through the house at full throttle yelling and screaming, not because he's angry or upset but simply because it's his way of expressing excitement. For him, yelling and screaming are part of having fun. His parents aren't amused. They wish he would slow—and quiet—down. Again and again, they have scolded and punished him for his noisy, frenetic behavior, without lasting results.

One afternoon Jimmy careens into the living room, ricocheting off furniture and screaming at the top of his lungs. His father slams down his newspaper and grabs him. "Jimmy," he barks, "how many times have we told you not to run through the house yelling like that?!" He gives Jimmy a swat on the behind. "If you want something to yell about, yell about that!" Jimmy runs off crying. For two whole days, he doesn't careen through the house screaming. On the third day, he resumes.

New scenario: Dad tries the "decoding" approach. Jimmy dashes into the living room screaming. Dad gets up, takes his hand, and says in a controlled but firm voice, "Jimmy, you're out of control, and you don't listen. I'm going to help you learn how to listen and stop running and screaming in the house. C'mon, let's go to your room and talk." Dad leads Jimmy into his room and sits him down on the bed. Jimmy protests. He thinks he knows what's coming. "I won't run and scream, Daddy! I won't do it anymore!" he promises.

"We're just going to sit here on the bed until you're ready to listen to what I have to say," Dad continues. It takes a little while, but when Jimmy settles down and is quiet, Dad resumes. "Good, Jimmy, I can see you're settling down and controlling yourself. Now . . . I know you were having fun running around and screaming in the house. You can do that in the backyard or in the park, but in the house there are going to be some new rules about running and screaming," says Dad. "After I've told you about them, you can leave the room. From now on, if you yell and scream and run in the house, Mom or I will take you to your room. The first time we have to do it, you'll stay here for five minutes. The second time we have to do it, you'll stay here for ten minutes. The next time, it'll be fifteen minutes, and so on. If we have to keep bringing you here, it'll make us sad, because you'll lose a lot of good play time. So I hope you won't do that to yourself. Do you understand?" Jimmy agrees and is allowed to leave.

The following day, Jimmy starts to run and yell inside the house, but catches himself and slows down. Dad congratulates him. "That was really good, Jimmy," he says to the boy. "Because you stopped yourself, you don't have to go to your room. But the next time you yell and scream in the house, you'll have to go to your room whether you stop yourself or not. I hope we don't have to do that to you."

During the ensuing days, both Dad and Mom regularly praise Jimmy if he is following the rules. "We're really proud of you," they exclaim. "You're really controlling yourself and not running and screaming in the house." If and when Jimmy fails to follow the new rules, the stated consequences are meted out. Remember, rules like these, when placed in effect, must be followed to the letter. They must become a real household priority, and that can mean cutting short a telephone conversation or stopping meal preparations to enforce them.

Jimmy's father is firm, but calm and supportive. He shows that he understands Jimmy's feelings and motivations. His tone is neutral, not critical. He simply states the rules and what will happen if they are not followed. Then he tosses the ball into Jimmy's court, making it clear that it's up to the boy to avoid the consequences.

Finally, why have I prescribed consequences rather than incentives in this example? I believe most parents find this kind of loud, frenetic behavior so annoying and disruptive inside the house that stronger steps are in order. Children like Jimmy need to feel the empathic power of their parents if they are to curb their out-of-control behavior.

## Jenny the Whiner

This eight-year-old has her parents at their wits' end. When things are going her way, she's fine. But when they aren't, she cries and whines inconsolably. It's been going on for years now, and if anything, it's getting worse. "Time for your shower, Jenny," calls Mom one evening. "Nooooo, I don't want to take a shower!" Jenny howls. Her parents know what's coming. "Stop whining!" shouts Dad. "You're acting like a baby!" Mom chimes in. "You're driving us both crazy!"

Now imagine a new approach to changing Jenny's deeply entrenched behavior patterns. Remember what I said about the need for all family members to be "on the same page" when applying the principles described in this book? In this revised Jenny scenario, Mom and Dad have talked it over and agreed on a course of action. This time, well before shower time, Mom says in a supportive tone, "Jenny, your dad and I want to help you learn how to stay in control of yourself when things don't go your way. Being in control of yourself means not crying and whining when you're upset. We can start right now, and I want you to listen to us. It will just take a minute to tell you." "There's going to be a new rule," Dad continues. "If you lose control of yourself tonight and keep crying and whining when we ask you to take your shower, there will be no play date tomorrow with your friend Sandra. We know that's hard to hear, but we also know that you need to learn to control yourself. So let's start now. We really love you, and we think you can do it."

If Jenny controls herself before her shower, praise and hugs are in order from both parents. Similarly, if it's clear that Jenny is *trying* to control herself, even if she doesn't fully succeed, both parents should say, in warm, upbeat tones, "I see you're trying! That's great!" This helps the girl recognize for herself better ways of expressing herself, ways that garner her parents' affectionate approval. Similarly, it can be helpful to question the child—not in the thick of battle but at some neutral time—about what, exactly, it is that upsets her about shower time. Does she dislike getting her face wet? Does the shower interrupt her play time? These feelings can be validated empathically by the parent, while still enforcing whatever new rules have been put in place.

Now, what if Jenny keeps right on fussing and whining? Then the consequence must be applied. And further consequences that have real meaning for the child must be employed as long as necessary, always described specifically and carried out in the same empathic, noncritical tone. Be patient and supportive, and avoid lecturing or any form of needless rambling. Make it very clear what the child must do to avoid a consequence—in this case, Jenny must stop crying or whining when she doesn't get her way. Again, consequences should not be discussed or treated as though they are a form of punishment. They are not; they are learning tools, and we all experience consequences of every description throughout our lives. Applying consequences teaches children to make choices for themselves, encouraging them to prethink their actions and to wrestle with their impulses in appropriate and ultimately constructive ways.

## Josh the Runaway

Now for one of the "worrisome" incidents I talked about earlier: the surprising behavior that seems to come out of nowhere and leaves parents wondering if something is terribly wrong with their child.

Josh is a nine-year-old who seems happy and well-adjusted. He rarely behaves provocatively. Then, one day, he declares that he's running away. He has his jacket on, and he's filled his pockets with crackers and other munchies from the kitchen. "I don't want to live here anymore," he says glumly, and starts out the front door. Mom and Dad, both incredulous, begin to laugh. "Don't make fun of me!" Josh exclaims, now angry. He slams the door behind him. His parents follow and find him sitting on the front steps, fighting tears. "We didn't mean to make fun of you, Josh," they say, now feeling real concern. "Why are you acting so silly?"

A common parental tendency in cases like these is to belittle or dismiss the behavior as "silly." To Josh, it isn't silly at all. He isn't equipped to appreciate its irrationality or inappropriateness. To him, he's acting normally and responding appropriately to a problem he perceives as very real and serious. Instead, suppose the scene were to play out as follows:

Josh stands by the front door, threatening to run away. Mom says, "Josh, something must really be upsetting you. Your dad and I can't let you run away, because we love you too much, but we really want to know why you want to leave. Please tell us what happened."

Josh finally says, "You and Dad were talking in the kitchen this morning, and Dad said he didn't know how hard it would be to have three kids, and you said you didn't either. So I'm leaving so it won't be as hard for you."

Mom and Dad both hug Josh. "Thank you for telling us what made you upset," they say. "Now we understand why you wanted to leave, and we feel terrible that you thought we didn't want you. Sure, it's a lot of work having three kids, but all the trouble is worth it. We love you very, very much and would never want you to leave us!" And so on. This particular example may seem a bit "Brady Bunch," but the underlying point is that the parents take Josh's feelings seriously and don't dismiss or belittle them as "silly" or "wrong." In situations like these, parents should also add, "If anything we ever say upsets you, please tell us, even if you're mad at us. We'll always listen to your feelings and try to work out any problems together." Even when a child's fears seem completely inappropriate to you, remember that they're inappropriate from your adult vantage point, not from the child's perspective.

## Worrisome Sara

Sara is five years old. She functions well on many levels but makes "worrisome" comments frequently enough that her parents are concerned. On one occasion she said she wished she were dead. Another time, she declared, "My teacher's mean to me. I hate school, and I'm not going anymore." Her mother, in typical fashion, hides her apprehension and replies, "Oh, you don't really mean that, Sara! You like school!" "Don't talk like that," her father chimes in. With an annoyed look, Sara retorts "I *do* mean it," and leaves the room.

Here again it's imperative that parents react to the

expressed feelings of children seriously, not dismissively. Applying the principles outlined in this book, a better response from this mother and father, both of whom are aware that their daughter makes worrisome pronouncements like these with some regularity, might sound like this:

"Sweetheart," Mom begins, "you say things like that when you're very unhappy about something. Let's see if we can figure out what's making you unhappy so we can help you feel better." Mom now begins to think about what events might have triggered Sara's remark. "Did something go wrong today in school? Did your teacher tell you to stop doing something?" she asks. "Did something happen here at home that made you sad or mad so you couldn't enjoy school?"

If Sara answers, then Mom discusses her feelings with her, reassuring and consoling her. Sometimes it can take considerable time and patience to uncover what's really bothering a five-year-old. Sara might have responded "I'm *not* unhappy!" to her mother's first statement, and hotly denied that anything had gone wrong that day. But Mom's effort is still worthwhile, even if the child never admits to the source of the upset. Sara will benefit simply from knowing that her mother and father take her emotions seriously, that they truly care about how she feels.

She will also benefit from beginning to understand that her emotions about one aspect of her life can be affected by some other, largely unrelated issue or experience. She can have a bad day at school because she's mad at her dad or her brother, or worried about something she overheard her grandmother say. In time, children like Sara open up more and more as their parents continue to demonstrate that such openness is safe for them and will engender serious, caring discussion, not judgmental lecturing or belittlement.

## Even More Worrisome Harry

Ten-year-old Harry has been in his room even longer than usual. He is frequently provocative with his parents. His mother looks in the door and suggests that Harry go outside for a while to get some air and ride his skateboard. "I don't want to," he mumbles. His mother grows more insistent. "No! Leave me alone!" he orders. Mom pursues it. "What's the matter, Harry?" she asks. "What's bothering you?"

"Look, I don't like my life," he replies. "I know you don't believe me, and you're just going to tell me I like to be dramatic. But I mean it."

"Oh, I am so tired of this!" Mom exclaims, heaving a great sigh. "You're so lucky in so many ways! You have advantages and opportunities all around you! And to you, nothing's right! Nothing's enough! We've *failed* you!" Dad, hearing his wife's agitated voice, enters the fray. From the next room, he calls out, "Harry, stop upsetting your mother!"

Interactions like this are utterly unproductive, and therefore do real harm. Regardless of the extent of Harry's difficulties, he needs help, and the parents aren't providing it by venting their own frustrations and speaking just as provocatively as their son. Further, children who frequently behave provocatively tend to hold on to their negative feelings. It's more difficult and takes more time to pull them out of angry or despondent moods.

In any case, a better response to Harry's declaration that he doesn't like his life would be something along these lines: "Honey, you're a great kid in so many ways that it makes me very sad and concerned to hear you say that you're unhappy with your life. I hope we can try together to help you feel better, because we love you very much. Can you tell me why you're feeling so unhappy now?"

Sometimes, of course, statements like Harry's are made in response to an obvious unpleasant reality, like an impending divorce. In such a case the parent might ask the child directly if that's the problem, and then discuss openly and in detail the sadness and uncertainty associated with it. As often as not, however, the source of the unhappiness is not so readily evident to the parent. In this instance, Harry may refuse to discuss what's bothering him altogether, especially if he feels that past attempts have been met with ridicule or belittlement of the magnitude of the problem. Children and adults see things very differently, as a result of differing life experience and a host of other developmental factors. Parents need to make the considerable effort to empathize with their children's problems in the context of *their children's* perception of them.

To be sure, an adult's perspective on some family or social issue can be very helpful to a child, but it must be presented in a way that still respects and validates the child's feelings, however inappropriate they may seem. How can we expect a child, with only a fraction of our life experience, to deal with his or her emotions and daily trials with the same effectiveness we do—or even to recognize what's truly worth being upset about in the first place? Even adults waste a lot of time and emotional energy fretting about things that really shouldn't concern them!

Returning to Harry, imagine that you're his parent and that he refuses to divulge the source of his unhappiness. In that case, don't insist or overdiscuss it. Be prepared to set the subject aside and return to it later. Don't express frustration. Later on, if you have an idea what's on the child's mind, broach that subject and see if you can start a discussion. Does he feel he's not getting enough love or attention at home? Did something go wrong at school? Did he receive a poor grade or have a fight with a peer? Sometimes children Harry's age appear so self-sufficient that their parents conclude, consciously or subconsciously, that they don't require as much emotional support as they did when they were younger. Meanwhile just the opposite is the case.

If your best guesses about the source of the problem produce no progress, then say, in a warm and caring tone, "I can see you don't want to talk about it, and that's okay. But I'm going to keep trying to help you feel better, because I love you and it makes me sad when you're unhappy. Maybe tomorrow we can talk about whether any of the things I just mentioned are bothering you." Be patient. If the child says, "I don't want to talk about it tomorrow," just say, "Well, if you're still sad then, I may try, because I care about you and I really want to help you feel better." Or you can simply say, "If you change your mind, you know I'll be ready to listen."

Sometimes it may be necessary to use an incentive to prod a child like Harry into being more communicative. If and when the source of the unhappiness is uncovered, the child can be urged to continue to interact. Of course, it's also necessary to offer sincere help in resolving the problem once it's uncovered. That may mean setting aside more "quality time" for the child, offering thoughtful advice on interpersonal issues, and even recognizing and controlling provocative behavior of one's own. It's every bit as important to analyze unflinchingly one's own possible contribution to the problem as it is to analyze the child's state of mind. An apology may be in order before all this is over! Remember, nobody's perfect, and that includes you!

Finally, if you are unable to uncover exactly what's bothering your child, that's okay, too. It is far more important that you simply demonstrate that you care, that you are available and ready to offer help if and when it is requested. Parents often underestimate the power of empathy itself. It isn't imperative that parents understand and discuss all their children's problems with them. Most kids resist this to one degree or another anyway. But children do need to know that their parents respect their feelings, sympathize with them when they're hurting, and can be counted on for loving reassurance and support. Merely asking Harry on the following day if he is feeling better says to the boy "Your mom and dad remember that you were unhappy yesterday, and we want to know how you're doing now. That's because we love you and care about you."

## Bossy Janice

Janice is ten years old and usually well-behaved. But she has an occasional tendency to "lay down the law" in a bossy, imperious tone. This rankles her parents and sometimes her peers as well. One afternoon her mother enters her room to put away a stray toy. "Mom, I don't want you in here!" Janice declares. "This is *my* room!" Mom loses it. "Don't tell me where I can and can't go in this house!" she snaps. "Who do you think you're talking to?!"

Now imagine the same scenario with a new response from Mom. This time she controls her temper and calmly replies to bossy Janice, "Well, something must be awfully wrong for you to talk to me in such an unfriendly way. Let's see if we can figure out why you're so upset." Now imagine that Janice—who, you'll remember, is usually well-behaved—replies in a conciliatory way. "I don't know why I talked that way," she says. "Sorry."

"Thanks for apologizing," Mom replies. "I'm very proud of you for doing that. Apology accepted." You may be thinking this is pie-in-the-sky again, but kids who are usually well-behaved often respond with an apology if their parents habitually react to provocation in a supportive, empathic way rather than in anger. To be sure, such a conciliatory response may not be offered right away, but it's common for it to come eventually. In this case, the mother ignored Janice's rudeness and addressed the meaning behind the words: that something was bothering her daughter. As discussed in the previous example, the mother does not pursue what the underlying problem might have been. By refusing to answer provocation with more provocation, the mother reveals the best part of herself, and her daughter reciprocates. The storm threat passes, and life goes on.

## Bossier Brit

Brit is just five, but don't cross him—at least some of the time. His parents are confused because his bossy tendencies seem to subside for a week or two, only to return just as aggressively as ever for no apparent reason. When they're at their worst, Brit is a real handful. One evening, after a period of relative peace, Brit's Dad asks him to pick up the toys in his room. "You do it! My arms are too tired!" Brit commands. "Oh, well, my whole body is tired, so get to it, young man!" Dad replies in a mocking tone. Brit folds his arms petulantly and declares, "You can't make me!" Jets of steam start to burst from Dad's ears. "Brit," he growls, "pick up those toys this minute, or you'll be in very serious trouble!"

By now I hope you're starting to anticipate how I would like to see a situation like this handled. Dad took a wrong turn when he responded to Brit in a mocking tone. After the boy complains that his arms are too tired to clean up his room, a better response would be something like this: "Well, Brit, I happen to know that you have very strong arms, and it would sure help Dad if you would pick up your toys yourself." Better to ask for help than simply make a demand in this situation.

Let's suppose that Brit still answers "You can't make me." Dad still needs to control his temper. Don't respond to provocative communication with more provocative communication. A better response from the father—*in a neutral tone*—would be, "Okay, Brit. I guess you want to be the boss about picking up your toys. That's fine, but I'm going to be the boss about this: If you don't pick up your toys, you'll go to bed in five minutes. That's how long you have to decide what you want to do. If you choose to go to bed early, that's okay with me, and we'll just leave the toys on the floor until tomorrow. If you won't put them away tomorrow, you'll go to bed even earlier tomorrow night. I hope you decide to pick up your toys so you can stay up until your regular bedtime. Five minutes . . ." Dad looks at his watch and walks away.

If Brit puts away his toys, praise is in order: "You know, I think you made a good choice," Dad might say. "Now you don't have to go to bed early." If the toys are still on the floor after five minutes, the consequence must be enforced, and escalated the following day if need be.

In response to the boy's initial bossy remark, Dad asked for help instead of issuing a direct order—a much less provocative course of action. But Brit still replied "You can't make me." So the father allowed Brit to be the decision-maker where putting away his toys was concerned, but he attached meaningful consequences to failure to cooperate (he knew Brit really disliked going to bed early). He was also supportive to Brit as he described the consequences, encouraging him to make the right decision—put away his toys and stay up until his usual bedtime. He was also fully prepared to follow through on the consequences if push came to shove.

## Hannah the Bossiest

This nine-year-old is frequently provocative. One day her mom picks her up at school. "Take me to the shoe store!" Hannah demands as she fastens her seat belt. "I want to get my new shoes *now*!" "Hannah, I hate it when you talk to me like that," her mother retorts. "You're very bossy and selfish, and I'm not taking you to *any* store today!" Hannah is furious; she complains vociferously all the way home, then sticks her tongue out at her mother as she disappears into her room and slams the door.

Now let's imagine an altered scenario, one in which Mom applies decoding methods and then consequences to encourage Hannah to gain better control of herself. First, Mom refuses to argue with Hannah in the car. That way, she can devote her full attention to driving. Instead of responding to her daughter's demands with a provocative rejoinder of her own, she merely answers, "Hannah, I know you really want your new shoes, but this is the wrong time to ask me." She then drives home without further comment. If Hannah provokes her, she repeats what she just said a single time, then ceases to respond.

At home, assuming Hannah is still angry and has stuck out her tongue and disappeared, Mom gives herself a few moments to calm down, then enters her daughter's room. "Hannah," she begins, "you keep talking to me as if you're my boss. You demanded that I take you to the store in a very unfriendly way, and when you didn't get the answer you wanted, you didn't say, 'Okay, Mom, I understand'; you argued and were very rude to me. You're going to have to learn how to control yourself. You're going to have to learn better ways of asking for the things you want and nicer ways of telling me you're disappointed or angry. I'm going to stop getting mad at you, because that doesn't help you or me. The next time you speak to me in a bossy, unfriendly way, I'm going to ask you to get control of yourself. If you don't try, then there will be no time on the computer for you the rest of the day. I know you can learn to control yourself, so I hope you don't make me take away your computer time."

Mom knew that Hannah loved to chat with friends over the computer after school and in the evening, so she was sure this consequence would have some persuasive power. Notice that she did not propose to levy the consequence the moment her daughter makes a slip and speaks in a bossy tone. Rather, she promised to give a warning. Then, if Hannah failed to stop herself, the consequence would apply.

An approach like this should be tried for about two weeks. If there's no improvement, double the consequence—in this case, to two days without the computer. Later, a further doubling to four days may be required. Application of consequences continues until Hannah demonstrates that she can control her bossiness most of the time. Remember to praise progress. Occasionally, it may be appropriate—that is, it may "feel right"—to skip a consequence if the child has a slip in the middle of a period of consistent improvement. In such a case, the parent can say, "Usually, I'd shut off the computer now, but I won't this time because you've really been trying very hard to control yourself."

When levying a consequence, don't discuss it. Just say,

in a firm but calm tone, "You've just lost a day on the computer." If the provocative communication continues, say, "If you keep talking this way, there will be no computer for two days." Don't engage in an argument; don't enter the fray. That's what the child wants: a confrontation, or at the very least continuing "engagement." When you get into the habit of denying that engagement, you reduce the incentive to seek confrontation in the first place.

Now, suppose Hannah refuses to control herself and her mother sees no choice but to levy a four-day consequence. At that point it's usually best to confine her to her room for a while. If she screams and continues to argue from behind the closed door, ignore her. Don't respond to her desire for engagement. If she refuses to stay in her room altogether, it may be necessary to suspend additional privileges, like phone use or TV-watching, for an entire week or weekend. Most children, however, won't carry it this far. Those who do with regularity may need professional help.

## So You Want to Argue

Some kids just seem to love an argument. They're usually six or older, and they can become quite expert at expressing their point of view. In fact, I've spoken with parents who have felt guilty for insisting on something, simply because their small child managed to martial such compelling, emotional arguments against it. More often than not, the parent is demonstrably right and the child is wrong, but the parent becomes confused and loses sight of the real issues involved when confronted with the child's passionate objections.

To be sure, it should always be acceptable for a child to

"respectfully disagree" with a parent and to participate in equally respectful negotiation. But here, when I say "argumentative," I mean provocatively contrary and insistent. Let's look at three argumentative kids . . .

## John

"Mom, you don't know how to help me with my homework," seven-year-old John declares one evening. "You always do everything wrong." "That's not true," says Mom. "Yes, it is," says John. "You're sure in a bad mood," says Mom. "No, I'm not," says John. "Yes, you are, " says Mom. "You've been disagreeing with me all day." "No, I haven't," says John. "All right," says Mom, now getting angry, "that's enough. You're going to drive me nuts." "You're going to drive *me* nuts," John replies. And so on, and so on—this could keep going all night.

Now imagine what might happen if Mom doesn't jump into the fray so quickly. John declares that his mother always does everything wrong. Instead of flatly denying the accusation, Mom says, "Wow! I do? That must be very frustrating for you! Are you sure I *always* do everything wrong when I'm helping you with your homework?" John is generally not all that provocative, and so he relents a bit. "Well, maybe not *always*," he admits. "Just sometimes." His mother replies, "Honey, you're right. I probably do sometimes do things wrong. And I'm glad you were brave enough to admit that I'm not always wrong. It takes courage to admit that you were unfair to someone."

By refusing to become defensive in the face of John's initial provocative remark, the mother quickly defuses the situation and stops a potential argument in its tracks. She gives John an opportunity to rethink his statement, and because he is generally quite well-behaved, he backs down. Finally, the mother reinforces John's willingness to modify his critical comment. She helps him "use the best part of himself." At seven years old, John isn't always aware when he's moody, and he can't easily stop arguing when he's upset. Perhaps he did poorly in school that day and is embarrassed to tell his mother. Whatever the underlying cause of his provocative remark, his mother responds in an empathic way that quickly brings an end to the confrontation and even turns it into a learning experience for John.

## Jared

This highly verbal five-year-old behaves provocatively more often than John does. His parents have been having a lot of trouble with him lately. Everything seems to cause an argument—choosing what clothes to wear, deciding when and what to eat, putting toys away, and so on. One evening Jared's dad says, "Okay, kiddo, bedtime!" "I'm not tired!" Jared replies. "You've been up a long time," says Dad, "c'mon, pajama time!" "You never let me stay up!" Jared complains "That's not true," Dad replies. "It is so! You can't make me go to bed!" Jared declares. "Watch your mouth, Jared!" Dad warns. "You watch *your* mouth!" Jared returns. I'll leave the rest of this one to your imagination!

In this example, Jared is more aggressive—and daring—than the previous child. But consider what might happen if Dad responds to the meaning *behind* Jared's words rather than to the words themselves. "You never let me stay up!" Jared protests. "Well, I can see you don't feel like cooperating tonight, and you want to have your way," Dad replies in a neutral voice. "So I'm going to give you a choice." "You can't make me go to bed!" Jared exclaims. Dad ignores the remark and continues: "Jared, either you put on your pajamas and go to bed, or tomorrow there will be no T-ball game." "That's not fair!" Jared complains. Dad looks at his watch, saying, "I'm going to give you five minutes to decide what you want to do. When the five minutes are up, either you head for bed, or there will be no T-ball game tomorrow. I hope you make the right choice. Arguing with me won't do any good; it won't change anything."

The five minutes pass, and Jared trudges off to his room to put on his pajamas. If he hadn't, Dad was fully prepared to allow the boy to stay up late—and to cancel the T-ball game he knew his son was looking forward to. He would also have escalated the consequence the following day if bedtime brought on another argument. Finally, when Jared capitulated, Dad praised his decision: "You're making a very good choice, Jared. I'm proud of you."

What was really behind the argument in the first place? If Jared had been able to analyze himself and express his true, underlying feelings, he might have said to his father, "Dad, sometimes I just like to argue to see what I can get away with. You make a lot of rules, and sometimes I just don't feel like following them. I didn't want to miss my T-ball game, so I controlled myself. But I didn't want to admit that to you!" By refusing to argue with Jared, the father took all the power out of his son's provocations. He even told Jared that "arguing won't change anything," so a power struggle was largely averted. The boy was presented with a simple choice in a neutral tone. He saw that this was a battle he really couldn't win, and so he gave in—and his father praised his decision.

## Brianna

Now for a more extreme example. Brianna is eleven years old and in a disagreeable frame of mind with her parents and siblings much of the time. She sometimes has trouble getting along with her peers at school as well, though she does have friends and is a pretty good student. One day she comes home from school and announces, "Amy invited me to go camping with her over spring vacation. I want to go." "Honey," her mother replies, "that would be fine, but your grandmother is visiting us during your spring vacation, and she hasn't seen you in a very long time." Brianna loses her temper, insisting that it's not fair, that she wants to be with Amy, that it hasn't been *that* long since her grandmother visited, that on another occasion Grandma couldn't come to visit because Mom and Dad wanted to take a vacation, and so on. Mom loses her temper, too, declaring Brianna selfish and spoiled. Brianna counters that her mother is even more selfish and spoiled. A shouting match ensues, and Brianna runs out the front door, slamming it behind her. She doesn't show up until well after dinner. Her mother is beside herself with worry. Fighting tears, she scolds Brianna harshly when she arrives home.

In this confrontation Brianna's underlying feelings probably went something like this: "Mom, I don't know why I say such mean things to you, but I was very disappointed when you told me I couldn't go on the trip with Amy. I don't want to be mean to Grandma either, but it's very hard for me when I can't do the things I want to do."

Despite the legitimacy of these feelings, the fact remains that Brianna needs to learn to be less argumentative and to exercise better control of herself when speaking with her parents. In this situation, one that occurs regularly in this family, I would recommend putting firm consequences in place. Let's imagine how the scenario might unfold if the mother employs some of the tools we've discussed.

As soon as it becomes clear that Brianna is not about to stop arguing, the mother says firmly, "Brianna, you need to learn to stop arguing with me. You won't get along well

with other people unless you get better control of yourself."
Brianna resumes the argument, insisting that it's not fair that
she should be deprived of a trip with Amy. The mother refuses to engage in more discussion about the vacation. "Brianna," she continues, "I need you to listen to what I have to
say to you. If you won't stop arguing and listen to me without making a comment until I'm finished, then you'll have
to go to your room for a half-hour." Brianna continues to
protest. Her mother sends her to her room. Brianna angrily
slams the door behind her.

After a half-hour, the mother opens Brianna's door. If
Brianna still doesn't cooperate, the mother declares that she
must remain there another half-hour. She doesn't negotiate
and concludes by saying, "I'll come back in another half-
hour. If you're still not ready to listen, you'll stay here *another*
half-hour. I don't want to have to do that to you, so I hope
you'll decide to listen and stop arguing."

When Brianna finally does calm down, the mother describes some new rules: "Brianna, I understand that you're
very disappointed that you may not be able to go camping
with Amy. I know you'd really enjoy that. But Grandma is
counting on seeing you. I will call her and see if she might be
able to change her plans. But if she can't, you'll have to stay
home. I'm sorry, but that may be the way it will have to be.
In the meantime, you need to learn to stop arguing with me.
Today is Tuesday, and your sleepover with Vickie is this Saturday. If you don't stop yourself from arguing with me for the
rest of the week, I'm canceling the sleepover. That means either no arguing at all, or it means when I tell you to stop arguing, you stop right away. I'll even cancel the sleepover at
the very last minute if you force me to. It's up to you. I hope
you'll control yourself, because I know you're looking forward to Saturday night." If Brianna fails to control her argu-

ing for the rest of the week, or fails to stop arguing after receiving a single warning, the sleepover is canceled without negotiation.

Notice that there are really two layers of consequences employed here—a short-term consequence in the form of escalating time spent in the bedroom, and the longer-term consequence involving the sleepover. The short-term consequence is designed to seize control of the immediate situation —to stop the confrontation so that the long-range plan can be set in place and described in relative peace. Notice that the mother validates her daughter's feelings about the camping trip but also prepares her for the very real possibility that she may not be able to go. Remember, too, that for some children, time spent in the bedroom is not a meaningful consequence. You might consider having the child simply sit on a chair or at the kitchen table. Try placing a clock nearby to time the half-hour, and don't engage in discussion or negotiation. Your outward demeanor must be calm and empathic, but your inner resolve must be very strong. When you demonstrate repeatedly to a frequently provocative child that you mean exactly what you say and that the consequences will be carried out precisely as described without amendment, the child will begin to exercise greater self-control.

## Steamed Sherman

Kids who lose their tempers with their parents usually provoke the most angry responses. Sherman is seven years old, very verbal, and most of the time he's pretty good-natured. But when he gets mad, his face contorts and words that could boil water issue from his mouth. His parents wonder if their son needs an exorcism.

One Saturday morning, Mom enters Sherman's room. "Honey," she says, "it's time to get up. Your tutor will be here in a half-hour." "Go to hell!" Sherman retorts angrily. "I'm not going to see my tutor! Get out of here!" Mom's face reddens with anger. "Where did you get that language?! Don't you *dare* talk to me that way again! Now get up this minute and put your clothes on, or there's going to be big trouble around here!" Sherman yanks the covers over his head.

In a situation like this one, I would recommend an entirely different approach from the mother. Her angry response to Sherman's provocation, while understandable, nonetheless fails to address what's really going on and doesn't do anything to prevent it from happening again. Better to proceed as follows:

After Sherman's remark, Mom keeps her cool, remembering that Sherman is only seven and is usually reasonably well-behaved. "Well," she says with empathy in her voice, "you sound like you really don't want to see your tutor today. But right now, I'm going to try this again. I'm going out of your room, and then I'm going to come back. When I do, I hope you can say something friendlier to me than what you just said."

Mom exits, then returns. Sherman, feeling guilty, says, "I don't want to see my tutor." Mom replies, "I know you don't want to, and I'm sorry, but he is coming, and you'll have to see him. If you do a really good job today, maybe you can take next Saturday off, but not today. And I like the way you spoke to me this time much better. Thank you." Sherman reluctantly slides out of bed. If he hadn't said anything upon Mom's return to his room, she would have said something like "Sherman, if you had said 'Mom, may I stay in bed and not see my tutor today?,' that would have been much better. If you can learn to talk that way instead of getting so angry, that would really help. I know you can learn." Later, when the air has cleared, Mom returns to the subject and explains to Sherman that "Go to hell" is not an appropriate thing for him to say to his mother. She also describes consequences she will enforce if Sherman continues to speak to her so disrespectfully.

In contrast to the first, angry parental response, this new one acknowledges Sherman's feelings and offers him an opportunity to express them in a different way. The mother praises him for using more appropriate language, and she also tries to respond to his desires by offering him the possibility of a free Saturday as a reward for good work. Finally, had Sherman failed to use friendlier words with her, she was prepared to suggest the right words to him. The profanity issue could be deferred for discussion, because it deserved more time than was available at the moment. Further, Mom might not have known quite how to respond to Sherman's language; she might have wanted to think about it a bit. In such cases, it's fine to raise the issue later, after the air—and everyone's head—has cleared.

## Hotheaded Henrietta

This five-year-old approaches her father one afternoon and says, "I want some candy. If you don't give me some, I'll cut off your head, and I'm not kidding." Dad snickers. Mom, overhearing this, says in a somewhat alarmed tone, "Henrietta! What a thing to say to your father! . . . Where did she get that?!" she adds, with an imploring look at Dad. "You better give me some candy," Henrietta murmurs.

Once again, these parents are simply responding to their daughter's remark, not to the meaning behind it. A more empathic approach would have Dad replying, "I think you're trying to tell me that you're going to be very angry if I don't give you some candy." "Yeah," Henrietta replies, "I'll cut off your head." In a supportive but firm tone, Dad asks,

"Can you tell Daddy that you don't like it when you don't get your way, instead of telling me you'll cut off my head?" "I want the candy," Henrietta replies. "Well, that's a little better," Dad says in a light tone. "Now I understand that you just want some candy, and I'm not worried anymore that I'm about to lose my head!" Henrietta fights a smile.

In this new scenario, neither Dad nor Mom responds with shock when Henrietta makes her provocative remark (I'll have more to say about "disturbing" and "confusing" comments from kids a little later in this chapter). The father explains to the girl what she was really trying to say instead of responding with a provocative snicker of his own. He gives her an alternative way of expressing herself, then praises her, even though she didn't really rescind her earlier statement— she is, after all, only five. He then adds a bit of humor to "lighten" the proceedings. Children have a hard time listening to constant correction and criticism. Often, when parents take steps to lighten an interchange, their children become less defensive, the sparks stop flying, and real learning occurs.

## Angry Aaron

Aaron, age ten and frequently provocative, is listening to his mother's seventy-fourth lecture about his mistreatment of his sister and getting angrier and angrier. Finally, he shouts, "Shut up! Shut up! Shut up!" "Aaron!" his mother shouts back. "I told you that if you don't stop talking to me that way, I'm pulling you out of Little League for good! I can't stand this anymore!" "You can't take me out of Little League," Aaron shouts back. "And if you do, I'll run away! I hate you!" He rushes out the door, slamming it behind him.

This is obviously a more serious situation involving anger, but it should be dealt with in more empathic terms. Aaron is frequently provocative, and consequences are therefore in order. But the manner in which they're levied must not parrot the very anger that got Aaron into trouble in the first place. This mother needs to step back and reflect on Aaron's patterns of provocative reaction. Most often, he loses control of himself when he doesn't get his way. By recognizing a simple fact like this one, parents often manage to control their own anger more effectively and remain in better control of themselves and the situation. As Francis Bacon wrote more than four hundred years ago, "Knowledge is power!" Knowledge of your child's behavior patterns helps you react more calmly, consistently, and constructively when provocative behavior occurs.

In this case, self-knowledge would also prove helpful to the mother. If she recognizes her own tendency to lecture Aaron, she might respond more effectively, as follows, in a firm but calm tone: "Aaron, I realize I was lecturing you again, and I know you don't like it when I do that. But you are going to have to learn to control your angry talk. If you don't learn to stop saying 'shut up' and other angry, mean words, you're going to miss a lot of the things you like to do, like playing baseball, watching TV, and seeing your friends. I'm making some new rules. Every time you lose control of yourself, you will spend a half-hour in your room. That means if it happens three times, you'll have to spend an hour and a half in your room. I hope you don't do that to yourself, because you won't be able to use the phone, or watch television, or play with the computer, or go outside. It's up to you."

If the behavior begins to improve, then the consequence is a good one, even though the child may insist he doesn't mind it. So don't necessarily believe statements like "I love being in my room!" If you're getting results, it's working. Phones, TVs, and computers need to be turned off or disconnected. Such luxuries take the teeth out of any consequence.

If isolation in a bedroom doesn't seem to produce results, try sitting at a table, as described earlier. Don't engage in conversation with the child, and don't respond to complaints. Increase the duration of the consequence as needed. And finally, be patient. Give these procedures two weeks to a month to work.

Aaron's mother needed to exercise considerable self-control to keep from losing her temper. But shouting never produces long-lasting improvement. A firm but empathic response is the only kind that eventually leads to consistent behavioral change. Aaron's outburst was simply the result of his inability to control his temper. The best way he knew to make his mother stop scolding him was to yell at her abusively. Then he tried to scare her by threatening to run away. His mother, responding to the meaning behind his words, first acknowledged that she had been lecturing him, then set firm boundaries on his behavior, backed up by escalating consequences.

## Vanessa the Blamer

This eight-year-old is sweet-natured and loving, but she has difficulty admitting she's wrong. "Did you leave this food out, Vanessa?" Mom asks one afternoon. "Look! The ants have found it!" "You always blame me when something goes wrong," Vanessa protests. "Jason could have done it. He was in here, too." "It wasn't me! You know you did it, Vanessa!" her brother calls from the next room. Mom frowns. "Vanessa, you should tell the truth and not make excuses. I know you were the last person in here this morning." Vanessa, eyes downcast, says nothing.

This mother doesn't really lose her temper, but she makes it clear she knows who's to blame. Her response to the situation, while not excessive, does not employ the empathic methods that are far more likely to help her daughter learn to take responsibility for her own actions. Mom knows that Vanessa tends to blame others when things go wrong, so a more effective response upon discovery of the ants in the kitchen should have gone something like this: "Vanessa, I'm going to ask you a question that you may have a hard time answering truthfully. But you won't get in trouble if you tell me the truth. Did you leave this food out in the kitchen?" Suppose Vanessa still answers, "Jason could have done it." Mom replies, "Honey, I'm asking you if you did it. It's really okay. I just want you to be more careful in the future if you did do it." Let's suppose that Vanessa sheepishly fesses up. Mom gives her a hug, praising her honesty. "I'm really proud of you for admitting you did it and not trying to blame someone else!" Had Vanessa continued to waffle and duck responsibility, Mom would have persisted in her reassurances, even offering to ask again later if Vanessa wasn't ready to talk about it truthfully.

In this altered scenario, Mom tells Vanessa that she knows it may be hard for her to tell the truth—an empathic preamble that softens the threat and reduces Vanessa's temptation to become defensive. Instead of scolding her for trying to blame her brother, she warmly asks for the truth again, reassuring her that she won't get in trouble. This helps remove Vanessa's fear and opens the door to an honest reply, which earns a hug and heartfelt praise, along with a simple, brief reminder (not a lecture!) that blaming others is never the right thing to do.

## Luis the Bigger Blamer

"It's your fault I don't get my homework done, because you're always watching television, and it makes a lot of noise, and I can't work!" Luis says to his father one evening. "That's ridiculous," Dad protests. "You have plenty of time and quiet to get your homework done. Don't try to blame me! I don't like your attitude, young man! You're always blaming everybody else for your own problems." Luis keeps it up: "You're always yelling at me, too," he adds. "How am I supposed to do my homework when you're always yelling at me?"

Again, a more effective antidote to Luis's tendency to fix blame on others would be a more empathic response from Dad. A better reply to Luis's initial accusation would have been something along these lines: "Honey, I know it's not fun to do homework, and it's hard to admit you could have done some of it earlier. It's also easier to blame me for things like that, but I'll make a deal with you. The next time you try to blame me for something, I'm going to remind you that that's what you're doing. If you can admit that you're trying to blame me, if you can say something like, 'Okay, Dad, it's not really your fault,' then at the end of the week we'll do something special, like get an ice cream cone. I know you can control how you talk to me."

In this new scenario, Dad doesn't react angrily to Luis's attempt to blame him. Rather, he acknowledges supportively the boy's struggle to do his homework. He then tells Luis he needs to learn to stop blaming others, but he does it without shaming him. Then, with the promise of a trip to the ice cream store, he establishes an incentive for improvement. He even explains to Luis exactly why he's making the deal. At eight, Luis is old enough to understand and benefit from hearing the meaning behind his own words and the motives behind his father's actions.

# Embarrassing, Confusing, or Disturbing Provocative Behavior

Usually, behavior of the embarrassing sort—typically from children three to five years old—is not indicative of any deeper problem. It's just part of a normal developmental stage in which children lack the experience to gauge the impact and appropriateness of their words. Similarly, "confusing" or "disturbing" behavior—the kind that makes parents ask themselves "Where did *that* come from?!"—usually issues from the idiosyncratic side of every child's mind. Sometimes such out-of-left-field behavior causes laughter. Other times it can make parents fear the worst—that their child is warped in some strange and sinister way. Almost invariably, such fears are unwarranted. Confusing comments are only provocative in the sense that they leave parents feeling confused, too, wondering what, if anything, they should do. The child who makes a strange, confusing, or disturbing statement usually requires only parental understanding, not consequences. Some examples . . .

## Daryl

Daryl is four. During a family gathering, he suddenly drops his pants and says, in a voice loud enough for deceased relatives to hear, "Mommy, look! My penis hurts!" Mom, mortified, whispers, "Daryl, pull your pants up this minute!" "Why?" says Daryl. "Look at it! It hurts!" "I'll look at it later," Mom hisses. "Look at it now!" Daryl insists. "Stop it!" says Mom, giving Daryl the evil eye.

Daryl is too young to appreciate the social impact of dropping his pants in public and loudly proclaiming that his private parts hurt. At four, he has yet to develop many inhibitions, and he feels no shame or guilt about his body. He's proud of his penis, and of all his other body parts. There's nothing wrong with this. A better approach for Mom would be to remain outwardly calm and unruffled, pick Daryl up, and say, "C'mon, Daryl, we'll take a look at it in another room." After she establishes that everything is okay and reassures Daryl that whatever pain he's feeling will go away, she changes the subject, perhaps suggesting a trip to the toy box or to the kitchen for a snack. His focus redirected, Daryl forgets his penis and moves on. For a onetime occurrence like this, redirection of the boy's attention is enough, and the parent avoids shaming him.

Now, what if Daryl had a pattern of such behavior and regularly did things like this disobediently or defiantly? Then a response like the following would be in order, spoken in a firm, but upbeat tone: "Daryl, there's going to be a new rule. If your penis hurts, you can only show it to Mom or Dad when we're alone. You need to remember to do this, so I'm going to remind you whenever we're with other people." If Daryl still disobeys, escalating consequences would have to be employed until the behavior pattern is broken.

## Nika

Grandma gives her five-year-old granddaughter a big kiss. "Grandma, you're smelly!" exclaims Nika. Mom, looking on and suddenly feeling faint, sputters, "Nika! That's not nice! We don't talk to Grandma like that!" She directs a look of extreme displeasure at Nika, then apologizes to Grandma, who has walked away, obviously embarrassed and displeased herself.

No one enjoys moments like these, except perhaps in hindsight years later when the memory finally becomes more amusing than painful. Nonetheless, a more empathic approach to the incident would have Mom take her daughter aside and say, "Nika, I know you didn't mean to hurt Grandma's feelings, but it made her feel bad to be called smelly. Why don't you go over and tell Grandma you're sorry and that you love her." If Nika pouts and is reluctant, Mom keeps at it: "C'mon, Nika, let's try. It will really help Grandma." If and when Nika goes over and makes amends with her grandmother, praise and a hug are in order. If she refuses to apologize, then Mom does it for her, saying something like "Nika's not ready to say she's sorry for hurting your feelings, so I will say I'm sorry for her. I know Nika can learn to do it herself."

What Nika really meant when she spoke to her grandmother as she did was, "Why do you smell that way, Grandma? It's a funny smell. What is it?" She's too young to realize the dangerous ground she has ventured upon, too young to know that she should refrain from comment! Thus, instead of scolding Nika, Mom avoids making her feel guilty and instead encourages growth. She helps Nika find the words to apologize. She doesn't react negatively when Nika is reluctant. Even if Nika refuses to apologize altogether, the mother still avoids making her daughter feel guilty for what she did, but instead chooses words that gently urge Nika to be more mindful of what she says next time. Remember, the goal is to teach, not to shame or to punish. When children are shamed or punished, they hear and feel only the parent's anger and lose sight of the "lesson" supposedly being taught.

## Barry

Mom and Dad are eating breakfast in the kitchen. Six-year-old Barry walks in and declares enigmatically, "My brain made me do it." Mom, fearing the worst, asks in a suspicious tone, "What did your brain make you do, Barry?" "Nothing," Barry replies, and leaves the room. Mom gets up and immediately begins to search the house for the mass destruction she somehow knows she'll find. She enters the bathroom and there, on the wall, is a large crayon drawing of their house, family, dog, cat, and hamster. "Barrrrryyyy!!" Mom cries. "Come here this minute!!" You can surmise what happens next.

If Barry had understood his own actions and emotions and could explain himself, he would have said, "Mom, Dad . . . I wanted to see what it was like to draw on the bathroom wall, but I didn't want to get into trouble, so I made up the line about my brain. I didn't know that's what I was doing, because I'm too young to understand my own unconscious motivations!" Assuming Barry is generally a well-behaved child, a better response to his confusing statement would have unfolded as follows:

"My brain made me do it," says Barry. Mom replies, in a *neutral* tone, "Tell me about your brain. What did it make you do?" "It made me draw on the wall in the bathroom," Barry admits sheepishly. "I didn't want to, but my brain did." "Well, Barry, I think it's hard to just tell us that you wanted to see what it was like to draw on the wall," Mom says. "Maybe next time your brain tells you to do something like that, you can ask another part of your brain to tell you not to. Or you can ask Mommy or Daddy if it's all right. I'll bet that will work."

By encouraging Barry to explain his initially confusing comment, Mom prevents him from feeling defensive. He readily admits what he did. She then explains the meaning behind his words in a tone that doesn't shame him, but instead helps him learn to make better decisions in the future. It's no easy matter to control anger in a situation like this one, but the calm, supportive response I encourage invariably delivers a more lasting and reliable result—the reduction or cessation of undesirable behavior. If you need to, go to another room and calm down for a while before responding to provocative actions like Barry's. And if you do blow a gasket, be prepared to apologize later. I know this is asking a lot, but the results justify the effort.

## Bruce

This five-year-old poses a startling question to his mother one evening: "Mommy, can you divorce Daddy and marry me?" "You don't really want me to do that, Bruce," Mom answers. "You love your daddy." "Well, I still want you to divorce Daddy," Bruce insists. "That's not nice, honey," Mom scolds.

Here again, Bruce is really expressing a desire to have his mother all to himself—a common wish for young children. It's not that they don't love their fathers; it's simply that at certain ages, the attachment to the mother tends to be stronger. A better response from Mom would be something along these lines: "Bruce, you'd really like to have Mommy all to yourself, wouldn't you?" The boy would likely answer yes. "Well, I can't love you any more than I do. But if I divorced Daddy, he wouldn't live with us anymore. I think that would make him very sad, don't you?" Bruce would likely answer yes again. "Maybe we can say I'm married to both of you. Would that be okay?" Again, Bruce would likely agree. "Good!" Mom concludes. "We solved the problem, didn't we?"

Why doesn't Mom clarify the reality of the situation to Bruce? Why doesn't she tell him that she can only be married to one person at a time, that it's an adult thing, that she's happy to be married to Daddy, and happy that Bruce is her son? Because it's more information than a five-year-old needs. Bruce was simply expressing his deep love for his mother and his reluctance to share her with his father, whom he also loves. The Oedipal conflict he feels will resolve itself as he grows older. By avoiding making Bruce feel guilty about his feelings, and by offering a simple solution—a "double marriage"—she resolves the issue in Bruce's young mind. She also shows him that divorce would mean that Daddy would no longer live with them. Bruce realizes that this is not something he wants, and he is satisfied with a resolution that seems to make it possible for him, and his father, to love and be with Mom together.

## Things to Remember About Responding to Provocative Communication

Applying the principles outlined in this book takes a lot of practice and self-mastery. It's not easy for parents to control their tempers in the face of repeated provocation. But by responding calmly to children's provocative communication, by sharing with them the meanings behind their words, by engaging them in problem-solving, real progress can be made remarkably quickly. Incentives and consequences have their places, too, of course. Here's the basic approach in condensed form:

- Control your own anger.
- Try as best you can to decode the meanings behind your child's words, using Chapter 3 of this book as your guide.
- Respond firmly but supportively to the meanings behind the words, not to the words themselves, thereby helping

(continued)

(continued)

the child understand his or her own mind and motivations. If you draw a blank and don't recognize any meanings behind the words, that's okay, too. You will still make progress simply by demonstrating that you acknowledge and sympathize with your child's struggles.

◆ Look for ways to problem-solve together.

◆ Employ incentives and consequences as learning tools when necessary, without negotiation, excessive lecturing, or anger and without withholding love.

◆ Praise progress; don't reserve it only for perfection.

◆ Be patient. Give these remedies two weeks to a month to begin to work.

# Physical Provocative Communication

**U**p until now, we've been discussing verbal provocative communication. But what about the child who puts his whole body into it—by hitting, kicking, biting, spitting, or throwing things? These physical manifestations of aggressive impulses are no less normal than their verbal counterparts. It's simply what's called "primitive behavior." Kids learn to delay gratification very slowly, and they have only limited abilities to control their impulses. Further, their verbal development can be considerably slower than their physical development, so anger and frustration can come out as actions, not words.

By the time children reach age five or six, they have generally begun to exercise better self-control. They may tend to reserve their physical provocative behavior for siblings and friends while relying more on words with their parents. Unfortunately, a whack delivered to a brother or sister can upset a parent just as much as a kick to Mom or Dad's own shin!

Most parents accept physical aggression from very young children—whether hitting, biting, or throwing—without reaction. They understand that their baby boy or girl isn't old enough to exercise restraint. But if the behavior persists much past the toddler years, parents become less and less tolerant. The child who remains physically aggressive past the age of five or six often has had a crisis of some kind to deal with—a divorce, a death in the family, a serious illness. In other instances, frequent use of physical punishment within the family is the root cause. Temperament can also play a role, as can slower-than-average emotional development. Often, too, parents respond to physical provocative behavior in ways that perpetuate it. More on this shortly.

Physical provocative behavior appears most often in response to not getting one's way: a little boy slams his bedroom door when told he must get ready for bed; his sister throws her doll in the birdbath when called in from play. Sometimes the behavior can seem downright irrational and outlandish, as when a child willfully damages a favorite toy in a burst of frustration or anger. Parents can find it especially difficult to stay in control of themselves in the face of such destructive physical outbursts. Some still administer spankings, which invariably upset the child even more and teach nothing except that physical violence is sometimes perfectly acceptable and that bigger people can overpower smaller people. Hitting a child back to show him or her "how it feels" is equally unproductive.

Other parents attempt to talk the child out of the behavior, but an out-of-control child hears very little, just as an out-of-control adult is unlikely to derive much benefit from a didactic lecture. Parents also typically become worried when their child appears out of control. They wonder if there's something wrong. Except in rare instances, there isn't. It's normal for kids to lose control of themselves. It's part of growing up. Nonetheless, an important key to putting a stop to your child's physical provocative behavior is to *remain in control of yourself*. When you get physical, you're modeling the very behavior you want to eliminate!

## Toddler Hitting

Toddlers often express displeasure, and even a sort of perverse curiosity, by slapping their parents on the face or leg. Sometimes, when the parent reacts with surprise, the toddler smiles, taking simple pleasure in creating a reaction. "When I hit Mommy, it surprises her!" the toddler might say if she could. "This is fun!"

The first step to take when a toddler delivers a slap is to ignore it. Say nothing. The child can't hurt you. Many toddlers will give up on hitting if it garners no reaction after several attempts. If the toddler continues to hit after you have ignored the behavior five times, move on to the second step: Say to the child, in a firm but neutral tone, "No hitting." Then put the toddler down and say, "I will pick you up one more time, but if you hit me, I'll put you down again." Repeat this for emphasis. Then pick the child up. If she hits again, put her down and don't pick her up again no matter how much she protests. Later, when you're about to pick her up, say, "Remember, no hitting." Then, if she controls herself, hug and praise her. Say, "You didn't hit! That's very good! I'm proud of you!" If the child usually hits your leg, you may need to devise a slightly different strategy, like taking her to her room if she continues to hit. Explain what you're doing and why: "If you can't stop hitting, you're going in your room until you can control your hands and keep them from hitting me." Leave the toddler in her room for about two minutes. If she doesn't hit when she comes out, praise her. If she continues to hit, say, "I guess you're not ready to stop. Let's go back in your room." Increase the consequence to four minutes this time.

If this approach still fails to work, move on to the next step, which is invariably successful. When your toddler hits, grasp his hands firmly and say, "If you hit, I will hold your hands until you learn not to hit." Hold on for about a minute, then let go. If the child still hits, hold his hands for two minutes. Say, "Honey, I don't want to hold your hands, but I will until you learn to stop hitting." Toddlers don't like being controlled in this way; they would rather control themselves than let you do it for them! When the child does not hit again upon being released, praise and hug him warmly.

## Preschool and Older Hitting

When preschoolers hit, it's usually a bit more serious than when toddlers do it, simply because preschoolers are strong enough to hurt you! It's normal for kids this age to harbor feelings of grandiosity—that is, they like to imagine that they're more powerful than they actually are. Also normal is the occasional acting out of these grandiose feelings through physical aggression. Further, preschoolers lack the experience and self-awareness to judge very accurately when their hitting crosses the line from play into real hurtfulness. Often they don't realize how hard they've struck someone until their victim reacts in pain or starts to cry.

Older children, ages six to eleven, have a much better

idea of how hard they're striking someone and whether it's going to hurt or not. When these school-age children resort to physical aggression, it's because they're unable to control their emotions and impulses and lack tolerance for frustration. This can have a wide variety of root causes. It can simply be a part of a child's basic temperament. It can also be the result of scores of environmental factors, from overcontrolling parents who unwittingly foster resentment and pent-up emotions in their kids that finally come out as physical aggression, to "the wrong friends," who model aggressive behavior at school or on the playground, to characters on TV or in video games that solve disagreements with karate chops, swords, or guns.

Putting an end to hitting behavior in preschool and older children can be a one-step or a multistep process, depending upon how stubborn or ingrained the behavior pattern is. Since older kids can engage in real discussion with their parents about behavioral issues, a good place to start is to simply bring up the subject of hitting in an unthreatening tone—not when the child has just hit you or someone else, but in a calm, neutral moment. "You really are a lot stronger than you used to be," you might say, "so it's very, very important that you don't hit people, because you could really hurt them. I know you can hurt people when you hit them, because the last time you hit me it really hurt. Will you remember that and never hit anyone?" Sometimes, a few brief, but firm, remarks like this one can bring about marked improvement, especially in preschoolers.

The next incremental step is to give a hitting-prone child an "advance warning" when you see a situation developing that has provoked hitting in the past. For example, Jimmy sometimes strikes his father when informed that it's bedtime. So one evening, just after dinner and well before bedtime, Dad says, "Jimmy, later tonight I'm going to tell you when it's time to go to bed, and I want you to try not to hit." Hugging Jimmy, he adds, "I know it's hard to stop playing when you're having fun, but when bedtime comes, that's what we have to do. Remember, no hitting, okay?" With the hug, Dad lets Jimmy know that he empathizes with the boy's feelings. But then he reiterates the no-hitting request. This advance-warning approach can be remarkably effective if employed in the calm, neutral tone described. An incentive can be attached to the request if desired. "If you can remember not to hit at bedtime for the rest of the week," the father can offer, "on Friday, we'll go to the video store and get some cartoons for the weekend."

But what if you're unable to identify a particular situation that typically leads to hitting? In such cases, make a simple, brief statement about the inadvisability of hitting twice a day when there is no conflict under way or even threatening: "Remember, hitting hurts people and doesn't solve problems. We do not hit." Whenever there is a conflict, however minor, and your child does not resort to hitting, praise the behavior. Say, "Boy, that's great that you didn't hit, even though you were disappointed/angry/frustrated! I'm so proud of you!" This reinforces the desirable behavior your child has exhibited and encourages him to repeat it.

If none of the steps above produce improvement within a few days, it's time to move on to consequences. Because hitting behavior can be a serious problem, it's best to devise a more serious consequence for it. For example, if the typical first-offense consequence in your household is "ten minutes in your room," it should be doubled to twenty minutes. Again, pick a moment when your child is calm—and you're calm, too. It's crucial for these remedies to be employed when your son or daughter is ready to listen and you're able to speak firmly, but not angrily. Use words like: "Honey, because you haven't learned to control your hitting, there's going to be a new rule. If you lose control of yourself and hit someone, you'll have to go to your room for twenty minutes. That's longer than usual, but hitting hurts others and you need to learn to control yourself right away. I know you can do it. You're too nice a kid to hit people."

Once the consequence is in place, enforce it without hesitation or argument. If it does not produce improvement within a week, escalate and/or change it. Say, "Because you're still hitting, the next time you do it, you'll have to spend thirty minutes in your room. If you still hit after that, you'll spend forty minutes, then fifty, and so on. We won't start over each day or even each week either. We'll add ten minutes to wherever we left off. Do you understand? You must stop hitting, and you'll lose a lot of play time with your friends if you can't control yourself."

Remember to avoid overtalking. Younger children may need to have the information—and the consequences—repeated before they respond, but older kids will generally get the message sooner. As always, devise a consequence that's meaningful to your child and that lends itself to escalation if need be.

## Throwing Things

Toddlers and preschoolers are the most common practitioners of throwing. The youngest do it mainly because it's fun. It's an expression of power over the things around them. Toddlers delight in learning that they can exercise control over their environment—and can even project that control over considerable distances by tossing objects as hard as they can. As kids reach age four or five, throwing is still done in fun, but it's also more frequently an expression of anger or frustration. Whatever the reasons behind it, there are effective steps parents can take to put a stop to it.

First, try setting up a "throwing place." Get a soft foam rubber ball and find an area of the house where it can't do any damage. Then tell the child, "This is your new throwing place." When he tosses the foam ball as suggested, praise him. Then add, "Whenever you want to throw something, just come to your throwing place and throw the ball!" Three- to five-year-olds can also be offered a standard rubber ball and directed to a safe wall outside as their "throwing place." This gives them an acceptable alternative means of acting out physical aggressions.

If the problem still persists, try an incentive. Every day your child doesn't throw anything, praise him or her and bestow a small reward like an extra story at bedtime. Older kids can be permitted to pick their own reward—a special play date or a later bedtime, for example. As a last resort, consequences may have to be employed, like the ones described in the previous section on hitting.

## Spitting

This behavior is generally limited to the younger set, especially infants, who do it out of sheer enjoyment. They're pleased with themselves when they discover *anything* they can do. Toddlers and preschoolers more often use spitting to provoke or tease others. It generally garners a reaction, and that's just what they want. So the best way to put a stop to it early in the game is to ignore it. Remember, small children don't care that it's messy or yucky or dirty or any of the negative adjectives parents use to describe it. They enjoy it. They're proud of it—and it's all a normal part of their development. But they also enjoy a reaction from you, and when they don't get one, they often lose interest in spitting fairly quickly.

Another approach is to lead the offender calmly to the bathroom and say in a firm tone, "If you want to spit, you may do it into the toilet, but that's the *only* place you can spit." Urge the child to spit then and there. Then say, "Are you finished? Okay. Remember, this is the *only* place you may spit from now on." Kids generally find this arrangement sufficiently uninviting that they amend their behavior. If the spitting is really excessive and the child persists after you've tried these responses, a consequence may have to be employed. But one thing is certain: This, too, shall pass!

## Kicking

When infants kick, it's rare for any harm to be done. They're simply not strong enough to cause injury. But the legs of toddlers and preschoolers are powerful enough to break things and cause injury, so kicking behavior in these older kids needs to be stopped promptly. Proceed directly to consequences without the more benign incremental steps. For example, you might say something like, "Janie, you must use words when you're angry or upset instead of kicking. So there's going to be a new rule. Every time you kick something or someone, we'll have to cancel your play dates for one week. If you don't kick during that whole week, we can start having play dates again the next week." Young children don't have a very clear conception of what a week is and will ask repeatedly if it's over yet. It helps to make a chart marked with happy faces for each kicking-free day that passes. Remember, too, to praise your child after each kicking-free day.

A weeklong play date cancellation may seem like a rather harsh consequence for a small child, but kicking is sufficiently dangerous to warrant strong action. A similarly strong response is in order for any serious physical outburst like hurting a sibling, as we'll see below.

## Biting

When infants bite, it's sometimes out of frustration, but most often it's a simple expression of curiosity. Babies, ever hungry for new sensory experiences, wonder, "How does Mommy's shoulder taste?" Further, it's part of the normal human apparatus to occasionally experience aggressive impulses within the context of love. Infants are no exception. Odd as it may seem, when infants bite, it can be a primitive expression of affection. Toddlers, especially those whose speaking skills are a bit slower to develop, can bite out of frustration over not being understood. Fatigue, hunger, and anxiety can also be culprits. So can teething. But what to do about it?

First of all, try not to overreact when your child chomps down on someone. Parental overreaction to biting can scare the living daylights out of the "bitee" as well as the biter. As with hitting, never bite the child back to demonstrate "how it feels." This almost never has the intended effect. Better to remind the child not to bite when situations arise that have caused it in the past. Gentle, empathic reminders, even to young toddlers whose language skills are limited, can bring results with patience. "Honey, remember, no biting when Mommy picks you up or when your friend comes over" is often enough to nip the behavior in the bud. Incentives can be employed as well, with consequences a last resort. When the child gets through an entire play session without biting, say, "Boy, that's great! You didn't bite at all! You're really learning how to control yourself!"

Another effective approach for dealing with a chronic biter is to periodically separate the child from a playmate or sibling, taking him a short distance away to play by himself for a while. Say, "I want you to play by yourself for a little while to help you remember never to bite." This reinforces the idea and its importance. It's not a consequence, because it's not employed immediately after a child has bitten someone. Rather it's a forceful reminder, one that carries greater impact than a simple verbal one. If the child still bites, visiting playmates should be sent home. You'll need the cooperation of the playmates' parents. Say to the biter, "Until you learn not to bite your friends, you can't play with them. I know you can learn, but until you do, your friend will have to go home." A similar plan can be carried out by the child's teacher if the biting occurs in school. The child is separated from the other pupils or sent home early. In either case, it's important to express confidence that the biter can change his or her behavior. As suggested above, say things like, "I'm sure you can learn to control yourself, so we're going to keep trying until you do."

Like recurrent hitting and kicking, stubborn biting behavior should be taken seriously. It needs to stop promptly, so if parents must resort to consequences, they should be more stringent than usual. If your standard time-out is five minutes, make it ten or fifteen minutes for continued biting after admonitions and incentives have failed.

## Physical Aggression in Older Children

When older children, eight or nine and up, are physically aggressive, serious injury can result, and so the most serious consequences must be employed. Boys most often exhibit such behavior because our society grooms them to be more self-assertive, to not be "sissies." Further, as boys grow older, testosterone begins to influence their physical and emotional lives. Far more often than not, children who are physically aggressive come from families that are abusive or in some way chaotic. The media don't help, constantly glorifying violence and associating it with power, something all children want.

When older boys or girls are repeatedly and intentionally (or even unintentionally) too violent, parents should enforce maximum consequences immediately—that is, go directly to whatever you consider to be the maximum consequence in your home, without any of the usual escalations. The consequence must be described to the child in the same manner all the other consequences in this book have been described: with empathic concern and without anger or irritation, even though that may go strongly against your natural impulses. Take the child aside—or both siblings, as the case may be—and use words like: "It disturbs me that you can be so mean and vicious, especially when you're such a good kid(s) otherwise. But because you are fighting in ways that cause real injury, you will spend the week in your room when you are not at school. There will be no activities outside of the house, and none inside either, other than your home-work or reading. That means no TV, no visits from friends, no computer, no telephone. You'll have dinner with us, then you'll return to your room. If this behavior continues, we'll double that consequence to two weeks, then a month if need be. Fighting in this way is very, very serious, and it must stop." Be sure to pick a consequence that is very meaningful to the child in question. Don't lecture, and don't waver after a few days. Carry out the consequence fully, as promised.

Especially when excessive physical aggression is in-volved, outside intervention may be necessary. This option is discussed in detail in Chapter 15. Parents whose children are physically violent also need to examine their own behavior unflinchingly and evaluate it in the context of this book's teachings. Unruly households, in which the adults frequently model aggressive behavior, tend to produce aggressive chil-dren. This, too, must be remedied promptly if lasting im-provement is to occur.

## Things to Remember About Physical Provocative Communication

- ◆ In the vast majority of cases, physical provocative com-munication is simply a variation on the verbal kind. It's just another normal part of growing up, and the same basic remedies described throughout this book work ad-mirably.
- ◆ When the threat of physical injury is present, more seri-ous consequences than usual are in order.
- ◆ Physical punishment/retaliation for a child's physical acts of aggression are utterly counterproductive. They

(continued)

(continued)

may stop the behavior in the short term, but only out of fear, not as a result of any real learning or emotional growth. Invariably, the pattern of physical aggression returns. Striking a child says "It's okay to hit under certain circumstances." It says "When you get older, bigger, and stronger, hitting is permitted." Are these the kinds of lessons you want to teach your son or daughter?

# Provocative Communication and Daily Routines

Children's provocative feelings often arise from life's daily routines, the little jobs and rituals that create needed structure in all our lives but also involve responsibilities that young people, especially, may resent. In this chapter we'll look at some of the common reactions kids have to daily routines—from dirty looks and muttered complaints, to flat refusals to cooperate—and outline some effective strategies for ending the conflict. Remember, the first step must always be to control yourself before you try to control the situation. That means stop "losing it." It means stop spouting orders and warnings like a drill sergeant: "Make that bed, *now*!" "Pick that up!" "You're going to be late!" "You're going to make *me* late!" Your kids have learned to tune all that stuff out, or they hear only the anger and not the message. Remember also that children simply cannot learn and accept daily responsibilities overnight. It takes them awhile. If you keep this in mind, perhaps you'll be a bit more patient. They *will* learn. If you make teaching them a shared family priority, and teaching them in the empathic ways I describe, they *will* change.

## Rise and Shine!

What parent hasn't entered a child's room a half-hour before the school bus departs and found an irritable, drowsy sack of potatoes under the covers? "I hate school," the sack declares. "Leave me alone. I'm too tired." If this is a recurrent problem in your family, the first step is to address it the night before, not at seven A.M. Say calmly and without irritation, "There are going to be some new rules tomorrow morning. I know it's very hard for you to get up before school, but we have to stop arguing about it every morning. So from now on, I am not going to ask you to get up more than two times. If you don't get up right away after the second time I've asked, you'll automatically have to go to bed a half-hour earlier that night. If that doesn't help after two weeks, then you'll have to stay home on Saturday, even if that means missing your soccer games. If you follow these rules, then nothing will happen at all, except that we'll have no more arguments in the morning. I hope that's what you choose to do." Pick consequences that affect your child's self-interest. Kids learn best when their self-interest is at stake. Enforce and escalate the consequences, as required, without negotiation or discussion. You may also want to reflect on whether your child needs more sleep in general.

## The Morning Coma

Some kids manage to sit up in bed when the alarm goes off, but then enter a strange catatonic state in which they make very little further progress. Teeth aren't brushed. Clothes sit in the drawer, untouched. Breakfast gets cold. The parents shout things like "What are you doing?!" and "You should have been ready a long time ago!" The child remains lost in the fog.

Once again, deal with the problem the night before, not at dawn. Say, "We have to stop all the slowness in the morning before school. So there are going to be some new rules. I will not tell you more than two times to get going or to hurry. I won't follow you around anymore. If you're not dressed in time to leave, I'll take you to school as you are, and that means in your pajamas if that's all you're wearing. If you're not in the kitchen in time for breakfast, you'll miss breakfast. If this doesn't work, then you'll have to start going to bed one hour earlier until you learn to get up on your own, on time. I know you can do it!" The majority of parents have taught their children that "new rules" aren't chiseled in stone. If that is the case in your home, it needs to stop. When a new rule is made, it must be enforced to the letter—calmly and without anger. Only then do children begin to see that they have a choice—a choice that is theirs *alone* to make: Will I follow the rule and avoid the consequence, or ignore the rule and suffer the consequence? There can be no doubt in their minds that a violation of the rule will trigger the consequence. This usually leads to some testing on their part. They probably concluded long ago that Mom and Dad only mean business when they raise their voices. So they'll need to get used to the change in their parents' disciplinary style. But when they do, they *will* learn to control themselves, and you'll be a lot less hoarse and frazzled.

Incentives can also be very helpful in lighting a fire under slow-risers. Younger children often respond to an On-Time Chart, with end-of-the-week prizes for five consecutive days of cooperation.

You may also induce older children to amend their slow-rising ways by simply taking them to school whenever they're ready, late as that may be. Don't get angry or lecture them. Just drop them off or send them out the door without comment. They will then confront the school's consequences for tardy arrivals. Again, this places the responsibility squarely in their own laps and forces them to make a choice.

## Bombed-Out Bedrooms

This is an area in which the child's perception of the situation is entirely different from the parent's. The kid feels that "it's my room and I should be able to keep it any way I like." The parent's response is "Who *bought* that room and everything in it?!" Most kids have a much, much higher "mess threshold" than adults. They seem oblivious to disorder. In my opinion, the tidiness of a child's room should not be too big an issue. Some parents learn simply to keep the door closed—out of sight, out of mind. But for many, it's very hard to ignore a bedroom that looks like a landfill.

Start by assessing the rest of the house, and in particular, your own bedroom. Is it neat? Don't be a "Do as I say, not as I do" parent. Children are supremely sensitive to hypocrisy. Assuming your bedroom looks like a page out of *House*

*Beautiful,* resist the urge to nag your messy child. It doesn't work, and you know it. Establish a regular pickup period at the end of the day, and remain in the child's room to see that it's observed. If it is, praise the child for the effort. If it's not, use empathic consequences, calmly explaining the whys and hows. For example, toys that have not been put away can be placed off-limits for a day (some parents call this "toy jail"). Kids younger than five will usually need a bit of help with the picking-up. Older than five, they should be able to manage it alone, though you may need to help them select appropriate storage places for their possessions. Frequently, kids really don't know where their stuff belongs!

Children who are generally well-organized and who exhibit good self-help skills should be cut a bit of slack in the room clean-up department, in my opinion. It's okay to lend them a hand as they put things away. Say, "Because you do a great job with so many other little jobs around the house, I don't mind helping you clean up your room." This reinforces the other desirable behaviors and also encourages such children to further expand their autonomy. On the other hand, if your child tends to be irresponsible, keeping a tidy room may be a good place to start building more orderly habits, and incentives or escalating consequences may be required.

## Mealtime

Many parents cling to an "Ozzie and Harriet" fantasy about family meals. They imagine their children politely passing the food around the table, conversing amiably about their day, their napkins neatly draped across their laps. Forget it! In the real world, most children see mealtime as boring. It's when they're obliged to make conversation, tell Mom and Dad "how school went," and endure long-winded lectures about what they're supposed to be doing and thinking. To make matters worse, they're required to down a procession of foods they often neither want nor like. Who would look forward to dinner under those circumstances?

In my practice, I tell parents to be realistic about mealtimes, especially with preschoolers. Be flexible about manners. Kids learn to eat more delicately as they get older, through observation of others and a growing awareness of whether they're out of step with appropriate social behavior. Concentrate on making mealtime a positive experience for your children. The younger they are when you start to do this, the better. The dinner table is the wrong place to lecture or criticize. It's also inappropriate to prolong meals artificially, insisting that children remain at the table well after they've finished, waiting for the adults to finish, too. I believe that fifteen or twenty minutes at the table is enough for children up to ten years old.

Model a happy, friendly mood yourself. It's catching. Ask children about their day, but be specific. "What did you do in school?" is a boring question for kids. It's far too vague. Instead, ask about specific friends, activities, projects, or teachers. For example, ask a child who loves to paint if she did any painting that day. This requires an ongoing engagement with the particulars of your children's lives. The more you know about what interests and occupies your kids from day to day, the better communicator you'll be as a parent—and the more your children will value your input, even though they may not readily admit it.

If and when children are openly provocative and rude at mealtime (including expressing their dislike for specific food items in discourteous ways), don't react provocatively yourself. Say, "If you can talk in a friendlier way, I will listen to what you're trying to tell me." If the child responds favorably, praise the effort. Say, "That sounded much nicer. Thank you." If not, and if provocative behavior at mealtime has been a continuing problem, say, "I'm sorry, but you're going to have to finish your dinner by yourself. It makes me sad, because we like you to be with us. But we've given you a chance to change your unfriendly way of talking, and you haven't done it." Send the child to his or her room, or some other separate area, with any remaining food. Later, tell the child that the same consequence will occur whenever such unfriendly behavior is exhibited at mealtime. Do not raise your voice. By refusing to become upset, you remove all the power from the provocation.

Finally, many parents have daily confrontations with their children about finishing what's on their plates. I advise mothers and fathers against making such an issue of it. Children do not willingly starve themselves. Even the most bizarre and picky childhood eating habits are essentially normal and almost invariably fade with time. Don't turn the green beans into a battleground; avoid that power struggle. Instead, calmly encourage your children to eat sensibly. When and if they do, praise them. If they don't, try to be patient.

## Homework

First- or second-graders who receive their first homework assignments are usually thrilled. Homework makes them feel so *big*! They get to take out their books and papers and pencils at home as Mom and Dad beam and offer a chorus of encouragement. It hasn't dawned on them that this will be a nightly ritual, one that will inexorably increase in difficulty and duration, for the next fifteen years of their lives.

By the time these same children have reached fourth or fifth grade, they've often started to whine at homework time, making regressive declarations like "I can't do this," "It's too hard," and "Will you help me?" Parents frequently respond with provocative comments of their own, like "If you don't do your homework, you'll never get anywhere!" Later, of course, comes middle and high school, where homework time can degenerate into all-out war. What to do?

Obviously, it's important to determine whether your child really does need extra help with assignments. If so, then it may be appropriate for you to provide it yourself or to arrange for extra tutoring. But if the problem seems to have more to do with unwillingness than inability, you'll need to take different steps.

First of all, parents should remember that homework is not a life-and-death issue. It's important to remain calm as homework problems are addressed, because these tasks are already stressful enough for your child. Don't add more pressure. Speak in an encouraging tone, not an impatient one. When children react regressively to homework, declaring they can't do it, that it's too hard and they need your help, acknowledge their feelings even though all the whining is exasperating to you. Say, "I know it's not fun to have all this work, but if you just do it, you'll be finished all that much sooner. Then you can do whatever you like." If the child is unmoved by this empathic approach and whines and procrastinates persistently, further action may be required. In a firm but supportive tone, offer the following pair of options: "Since you're having a hard time getting control of yourself, you can either stop fussing and whining and I'll help you get started for a little while . . . or we'll just go to bed very early and I'll send a note to school telling your teacher that you refused to do your homework. I'll ask her for suggestions. Now, which would you prefer?" You must be prepared to carry out the consequence. It's one that's designed to create a mild social embarrassment for the child, but I believe that's better than shielding children from the consequences of their actions. If the child says "I don't care if you send a note or not," so be it. Simply write the note. The vast majority of parents don't have to take the step more than once.

## Technology Wars

A lot of provocative communication can arise in connection with television, computer, and telephone use. TV and video games, as well as the Internet, all have addictive qualities. Many grown-ups have become "hooked" on these media, and kids are, if anything, even more susceptible. The telephone, too, can begin to occupy more and more of a child's free time in late preadolescence. Provocative behavior often takes the form of minimization and "little white lies" like "Mom, I've only been playing Space Pulverizer for five minutes!" If and when your child's use of the television, computer, or phone becomes excessive, specific limits on these activities need to be established. It's generally best to list such activities and time limits in writing—one hour of TV per day, thirty minutes of phone time, and so forth. Have your child sign the list. Set the limits in a firm but empathic way. Say, "I know you enjoy playing computer games, but you're spending way too much time in front of that screen. So from now on, we're going to have a new rule . . ." Set maximum limits as you see fit and enforce them, with a timer if necessary. If the child continues to be provocative after time limits have expired, you may have to resort to consequences.

In Chapter 14, we'll discuss in detail the effects of the media on children and parental responsibilities in that regard.

# Public Battles

Children's provocative behavior in public is one of the most difficult trials for parents. Almost every mother and father has endured a tantrum in a department store aisle or a screaming fit on a crowded sidewalk. Such displays traditionally elicit from parents a circulation-stopping squeeze on the arm accompanied by the most withering of evil eyes and a hissed warning that the known universe will explode if the behavior doesn't stop *this instant*. Threats like these, however, seldom do any good. Children younger than nine or ten are generally not particularly concerned about how strangers perceive them. Their desire to get what they want far outweighs any self-consciousness in public.

Of course, infants and toddlers have very little control over their behavior in general, especially when they're tired. Parents simply need to exercise care in deciding where to take them, or whether to take them at all. An exhausted two-year-old can't be expected to behave on an hour-long trip to the supermarket, for example, and a seat near the door makes sense in church, so that one can beat a hasty retreat if and when the crying starts.

Older children, however, need limits, and they can be set using the same kinds of incentives and consequences we've discussed throughout this book. If, for example, you have planned a trip to the store followed by a romp in the park, and have then threatened to withdraw the park visit because your child is fussing, you must be prepared to cut the outing short. Most parents go only so far as to pull the car over to the side of the road and threaten to turn around. But sooner or later it will probably be necessary to go "all the way." When a child is consistently provocative in public, it's worthwhile to actually plan an excursion that you secretly intend to cut short. Of course, if the child is well-behaved, do everything that you promised and praise the child for being so friendly and fun to be with. But if the provocative behavior continues, give one warning in a neutral tone, then calmly follow through with the consequence if it isn't heeded. Say, "Honey, if you can't control yourself and start speaking in a friendly way, we will go home without stopping at the playground. You'll miss having a lot of fun, so I hope you'll get control of yourself." Additional consequences may have to be added, like cancellation of play dates and the like, if steps like these don't produce improvement within a week or two.

There is one other step parents can take in especially stubborn cases. Sometimes it can prove beneficial to intentionally embarrass a child. Say to your son or daughter, "You were very loud and angry at the mall yesterday, and you wouldn't control yourself. If it happens again, I'm going to try something different. I'm going to apologize for you to anyone who is near us and tell them that you haven't learned to control yourself yet. I want them to understand that you're not a rude, unfriendly kid, but a very nice kid who needs to learn better self-control. I hope I don't have to explain this to people, but I will if I have to." Then, if and when the child is provocative in public and refuses to respond to your firm requests for self-control, do exactly what you said you would do. Especially with children nine or older, this kind of mild social exposure can be a very effective way to motivate behavioral change. Some parents don't like the approach, but I recommend it as a last resort when a child is persistently rude in public. Certainly, it is no more embarrassing than the public misbehavior that provoked the technique's use in the first place.

## Anticipating Prescribed Remedies

I hope by now you're getting the idea, anticipating the remedies I will prescribe after you've read about specific provocations. All this is considerably harder to do than it sounds, especially the requirement that you control yourself and your own temper, refraining from raising your voice or displaying excessive emotion when your children misbehave. But when you deprive provocative communication of its power by refusing to react to it in kind, you'll begin to see real improvement over time. That's a promise!

### Things to Remember About Provocative Communication and Daily Routines

◆ Kids need time to learn and habitually execute daily responsibilities. Be patient!

◆ Try incentives, like progress charts, before resorting to consequences, especially with younger children.

◆ If and when a consequence is employed, there can be no doubt in a child's mind that it will be carried out if the stated rule is broken. Only then will the child realize that the behavioral decision is his or hers alone to make.

(continued)

(continued)

- ◆ Your kids will need time to adjust to changes in your disciplinary style. If you've given your children reason to believe you only mean business when you shout, then they will have to unlearn that attitude before the remedies I prescribe can work.
- ◆ Don't be a "do as I say, not as I do" parent. If you require tidiness from your children, you must first be tidy yourself.
- ◆ When your children behave provocatively, their objective is to elicit a reaction from you. When you remain calm, you remove the power from their provocation and thus deter further provocation.

# Provocative Communication and Sibling Rivalry

The first thing to remember about sibling rivalry is that it's always going to be there, no matter what. Even siblings who get along well have feelings of rivalry; they've simply chosen to keep such thoughts to themselves, for whatever reason. Brothers and sisters who interact in unfailingly mellow fashion still compare themselves to one another privately, each wishing he or she were as attractive/smart/athletic/old/young/favored as the other. So sibling rivalry is normal and usually healthy, as long as it's kept within reasonable bounds. But in many families, provocative behavior among siblings gets out of hand regularly, and parents feel obliged to step in.

The most common expressions of sibling rivalry are verbal teasing and belittlement, hitting and shoving, and competitiveness that is not sportsmanlike, but instead aimed at showing off the inadequacies of the opponent. The more clumsy, hopeless, and stupid the other sibling is made to look, the better. Sibling rivalry also finds expression in interaction with parents, as in "Why can't I do it? You let *her* do it!"

Moms and Dads tend to fear the worst where sibling rivalry is concerned. They worry that their kids will never be friends, that their intense competitiveness and abrasive interaction will foster deep-seated animosities that will poison their relationship forever. Often, too, as parents observe their children's rivalries, they relive painful memories of their own youth and of being either victims or perpetrators in their own sibling relationships.

To make matters worse, parents understandably scold older children for bullying younger ones. "You should know better than to treat your sister that way!" they exclaim. "You're too old for that kind of behavior!" This causes the older child to feel picked on, and retaliation, usually directed once again at the younger sibling, takes place behind the parents' backs. If, on the other hand, the younger sibling is the perpetrator, mercilessly pestering his older brother or sister, parents often find it hard to understand why the older child becomes so upset. "You're acting like a baby," they may chide. "Just ignore him."

The fact is, normal sibling rivalry is *not* a deep-seated conflict about being "replaced" by a younger brother or sister, full of perverse envy, jealousy, and murderous musings. You'll find that sort of thing in Shakespeare's plays but not in the typical modern-day household. Older siblings generally have no serious fears that their "throne" is being usurped and that their rival must be stopped at all costs, nor do younger siblings have any serious desire to "take over" their older sibling's turf. Rather, most sibling rivalry is about the simple, daily conflicts that are bound to occur when a newcomer arrives on the scene and space and attention must suddenly be shared. "You complicate my life!" an older sibling might say to the newcomer if he could. "It was all much easier before you got here, so stay out of my way!" Most siblings do love each other underneath it all, even though that may seem hard to believe at times. They share powerful familial bonds. So it should come as no surprise when they have dramatic provocative reactions to one another, any more than it should come as a surprise when they play together amicably.

The bottom line is that parents and their kids often have very different perceptions of sibling rivalry and very different agendas as they try to deal with it. Parents may also be unaware of their complicity in the creation of the problem in the first place.

Consider two situations. Example number one:

A family has two brothers, ages eight and twelve. They're at each other's throats all the time, and the parents are having great difficulty dealing with it. One day, Mom is behind the wheel on the way to the market, and the two boys are in the backseat bickering. The eight-year-old has been needling his brother all day. Mom has repeatedly told them to stop it, trying not to take sides. Her warnings have fallen on deaf ears. Finally, the twelve-year-old exclaims to his little brother in a menacing tone, "If you don't shut up, I'm going to stab you to death in your sleep, and I mean it! I'll do it!" Mom freaks out. "How can you say such a horrible thing?!" she shouts. "That's a *sick* thing to say to your brother!" Then she turns on the eight-year-old. "And you should be ashamed of yourself, too! You just can't shut your mouth, and I've had it! The two of you should go off and live all by yourselves someplace!"

Interestingly, Mom and her sons are coming from two entirely different places here. Mom is horrified and angered by the older boy's stabbing threat. But the reality is that he threatens his brother in similarly lurid terms regularly, albeit out of Mom's earshot. The younger boy is used to it; in fact, his older sibling's threats of lethal violence generally incite him to be all the more annoying. The older brother knows this, too, but threatening to stab the eight-year-old makes him feel better. It helps him vent his frustrations. He knows that if he were merely to hit his little brother, he'd be in big trouble. So he's stuck with verbal threats, and they need to be good ones!

This is a classic instance of divergent perceptions and agendas. Mom is at her wits' end, deeply concerned that her children may be profoundly abnormal and in real danger. Her sons feel they're merely conducting business as usual. "What's the big deal?" they both wonder. And to make matters worse, the mother's loss of temper only perpetuates the very kind of unrestrained outburst that upset her in the first place; she is modeling loss of control, which is precisely what she doesn't want from her sons.

Example number two:

The father of a girl and boy, ages four and eight, respectively, enjoys playing catch with the older sibling. The younger one is less coordinated by virtue of her age, though she pleads to be included. The father insists that she play with her mom, and the older child chimes in, "You're too little. Dad and I are going to play catch by ourselves." After several such incidents, the girl begins to provoke the boy, calling him names, jumping on his back and pounding on him, and saying she wishes she had another brother. Both parents scold her and insist that she stop this behavior, with little effect.

The truth is, the father helped create the problem by excluding the four-year-old from group play with her brother. A compromise on playing catch (with cooperation from the older boy), or some exclusive father-daughter time to balance the father-son time, would reduce the girl's resentment of her brother.

Now let's look at some specific sibling battlegrounds and explore ways in which you can encourage a more lasting truce. As you'll see, handling sibling rivalry effectively begins with listening for the meaning behind the words, just as described in previous chapters. When the real issues that underlie siblings' battles are unearthed and addressed, more peaceful coexistence becomes possible.

## Bad Moods

Often, siblings tangle with each another simply because one or both of them is in a bad mood. Adults sometimes wake up on the wrong side of the bed, and kids do, too. When grown-ups feel cranky, their spouses are most likely to wind up on the receiving end. Similarly, when kids feel cranky, their brothers and sisters typically become the first targets for abuse. Kids' bad moods can be the result of a problem at school, a social issue, or a loss on the playing field. Hunger, fatigue, or boredom are often contributing factors.

When a usually cooperative child abuses a sibling, and your decoding of the situation suggests that a bad mood is behind the behavior, take the child aside and ask about it in a warm, helpful tone. "It's not like you to talk to your brother that way," you might begin, "so something must have put you in a bad mood. Why don't you tell me about it? Maybe I can help." If the child responds, praise her. With understanding of her own motivations will come a reduction in her hostilities toward her brother. If she doesn't respond, just say something like, "Maybe you can think about apologizing to your brother soon. It's not like you to behave this way, so I think you'll find a way to say you're sorry when you're ready." A child who is usually kind to siblings needs no more than this. Overreacting tends to foster more resentment toward the sibling, not less, because the child associates the sibling with "getting me into trouble."

Children whose bad moods are more frequent and who customarily take out their unhappy feelings on their brothers and sisters need a firmer approach with incentives or consequences. Make the same attempt to discuss the child's bad moods, but then set a timetable: "You need to learn not to take your unhappy feelings out on your sister," you can begin—as always, in a calm, firm tone, without anger. "You really need to come to me when you're upset, and we'll talk about it together. I'm going to give you a week to change your behavior. If you're still being mean to your sister after a week has passed, every time you use mean words when you speak to her, you will have to go to bed a half-hour earlier. I hope you won't do that to yourself. I hope you'll learn to be nicer to your sister." If you are persistent with this approach and carry through on the consequences as described, you will see improvement soon. Again, the key is to remain composed yourself. Your child must hear your *words*, not your anger or frustration. As in all the other situations described throughout the book, pick a consequence that is meaningful to your child and can be escalated as required.

## Winning and Being First

Another frequent sibling battleground involves winning or being "first"—first to the dinner table, first to the top of the stairs, first to the bottom of the stairs, first in or out the door. Kids are naturally competitive. Competition is fun. Winning also makes children feel important and successful, and they enjoy those feelings just as much as adults do. In general, competition is good for children because it teaches them lessons about winning and losing that they'll carry throughout their lives. There's no escaping competition, and we all need to begin practicing it from an early age.

Developmentally, it takes a long time for children to give up the need to win and be first all the time. Preschoolers can become very upset when they lose. By the age of eight or nine, most children begin to realize that others have skills they themselves lack. This is a painful awareness, but by fits and starts, kids slowly accept themselves as they are and give up at least some of their fantasies about being "the greatest."

When competitiveness turns ugly among siblings, however—with name-calling, belittlement, and rude gloating—parents may need to intervene. A child who rarely behaves competitively with siblings, or who frequently displays good sportsmanship in competitive activities, should not be chastised for a "slip." When such a child does become excessively intent on beating a brother or sister at a game or being the first to do something, one need only be a good observer and see how the children work out the competitive confrontation between themselves. Later on you can comment in an empathic tone: "I noticed that you and your brother had quite a race into the theater for an aisle seat. I'm really proud of you for not making a big issue out of it when he got there first." Or if the race didn't end quite so benignly, you can say, "You know, I hope you won't get into the habit of trying to race your sister all the time, the way you did in the theater. You usually don't, and I'm so proud of you when you're kind to each other and don't always try to be first." With kids who generally are not excessively competitive, this is often enough to keep them on track. Better to underreact, at least initially, than to overreact and risk worsening the problem.

When competitiveness gets out of hand regularly among siblings, more decisive action is required. Gather the children together in a calm, neutral moment—perhaps shortly after they've gotten up in the morning, when they're well-rested. Say something like the following in a firm but friendly tone: "Kids, you've been having a lot of trouble being good winners and losers when you play together. You argue about who's going to be first, you make fun of each other for losing, you accuse the winner of cheating. I think you know the kind of behavior I'm talking about. This has to change, and I'd like to see you try to come up with ways to get along better and be better winners and losers. An example would be saying 'good game' to each other, instead of 'you cheat!' or 'you stink!' or 'ha-ha, I beat you!' I'd like to see a real improvement within one week. After that week is over, if you're still not being good winners and losers, I'm going to call a time-out and you'll have to stop whatever you're doing for ten minutes [or twenty or thirty—whatever you feel is customary or appropriate]. If you're playing ball, I'll take the ball away for that length of time. And if you still can't be better winners and losers after that, I'll take the ball away for the rest of the day. I hope you'll do the right thing and not lose your play time."

Improvement usually appears in fits and starts, with a step backward for every few steps forward. Use your judgment about enforcing the consequences: If a child starts to be a "bad winner" but catches himself, praise him for recognizing the lapse and correcting it. In other words, be firm but flexible.

At the start of each new day, remind the children about the new rule. Say, "I hope I don't have to take away any of your play time." This demonstrates that you empathize with their feelings and wish for their pleasure—quite the opposite of the message behind a remark like "You'd better get along with each other, or else!" Escalate the consequences as required, using the same firm, calm tone.

If the competitive problems center on needing to be first all the time, give the children a week to engineer an improvement on their own, as described above. Then, if need be, establish a new rule like putting whoever tries to be first in last place for a while. As before, do this in a calm moment, not in the heat of battle. "When I see an improvement," you can add, "we'll all take turns being first and last."

## Teasing and Belittlement

One of the most common ways sibling rivalry is acted out is through teasing and belittlement. Older children are usually the perpetrators and younger brothers and sisters the victims, but as many parents know, the opposite can occur, too. As mean-spirited and unnecessary as this behavior seems, it's a natural part of many children's development. Teasing makes the teaser feel more powerful and important. It is sometimes an expression of revenge for real or perceived transgressions, which can include simply being born, or a belief that the victim is more loved or respected by the parents. A bad mood can be the culprit, too, and who better than a sibling to take it out on? On still another level, teasing has a component of fun, just as practical jokes have a component of fun—for the perpetrators, at least, if not the victims.

The child who makes a habit of teasing and belittling a sibling can almost never be reasoned out of it. The need for this kind of power is too compelling. Strong consequences are the only effective remedy. In a supportive tone, say, "It's important for us to teach you that teasing is mean and unacceptable, and you do it much too much. You're too nice a kid to say such mean things to your brother or sister all the time. We're not going to yell at you any more when you tease, but there is going to be a new rule, and here it is: Every time you tease your brother or sister, you will have to go to bed a half-hour earlier. If you tease your brother or sister three times, that means you'll go to bed an hour and a half early."

If and when the child teases a sibling again, say without anger, "You now have to go to bed a half-hour early tonight." Do not discuss the matter further or engage in any negotiations. If the child keeps pleading for a retraction, promising to stop teasing, say, "If you continue to try to discuss this, I will add another half-hour, and you'll go to bed a full hour early." Do not hesitate to enforce whatever consequence you choose to employ. A child may test the escalated consequence to see if you mean business. He must discover, to his chagrin, that you do!

## That's Mine! Leave It Alone!

Ownership and territory are among the most common sources of sibling rivalry. A child's room, toys, hobby supplies, computer, bike, private papers—all can be sacrosanct and off-limits to brothers and sisters. The fortunate parents of children who only rarely butt heads on ownership and territory issues need to refrain from intervening on the infrequent occasions when one child oversteps a boundary. Honor such children's rights to work out their own conflicts. If one of them complains to you, empathize with the child's feelings, but return the ball to his or her court. Say, "I understand why that bothers you. Ask your sister not to take anything out of your room without asking you first. She shouldn't have done what she did, but remember, she almost never does. I think she'll understand if you talk to her. If she doesn't, come back to me and I'll see if I can help." This approach demonstrates your support but gently encourages autonomy in conflict resolution, of which these siblings have already demonstrated they're capable.

If your child's ownership and territory issues cause frequent conflict, it's time for consequences. Apply them firmly but in a neutral tone, reminding the child that it is his or her choice whether or not they will have to be enforced. Consequences may have to be used with a child who constantly invades a sibling's space or toy box, despite being asked to stop. Similarly, a child who is unreasonably territorial and refuses to accept normal and reasonable forays into his room or belongings may need consequences as well.

## Don't Just Get Mad, Get Even!

Most children, when they feel wronged, want revenge. It's a natural human feeling, one that's been portrayed in literature for centuries. Ulysses wanted it. So did Hamlet. Even toddlers are liable to hit when they feel mistreated.

As in the earlier examples, children who only rarely seek revenge on their siblings should be encouraged to deal with it among themselves on the occasions when it does happen. Imagine a situation in which a seven-year-old is building a tower of blocks. An older brother walks by, carrying a toy of his own, and accidentally knocks the tower down. In retaliation, the seven-year-old knocks the toy out of the older sibling's hands. A tussle ensues and Dad steps in. Pulling the two apart, he reminds both of them how nicely they usually play together and encourages the older boy to apologize for bumping into the tower of blocks, even though it was an accident. Then he encourages the younger child to apologize as well. If either one refuses, the father says, "Well, maybe you can think about it for a while and say you're sorry later, when you're ready to. I'm very proud of how well the two of you play together most of the time and how well you solve your own problems." His tone is calm and empathic throughout. This kind of response is supportive of the children, encouraging them to continue their usually peaceful coexistence.

But what about children who engage in a constant, revenge-driven tug-of-war, each constantly trying to "get back" at the other? In such instances, consequences must be employed. Pick a relatively calm, neutral moment, and begin by explaining to the siblings your view of the problem, giving specific examples of the kind of behavior you're talking about: "Bobby and Mike, the two of you need to find friendlier ways of treating each other, rather than constantly trying to 'get back' at each other. For example, Bobby, Mike will poke you in the ribs with an elbow, and then you'll feel you have to poke him back, but harder. Then Mike pokes *you* back even harder, and it just goes on and on. Then, yesterday, Bobby accidentally knocked your jacket onto the ground, Mike, and you got back at Bobby by stepping on *his* jacket. You both have to learn new ways to solve problems between yourselves, because we don't want you to grow up being mean to each other. So there are going to be some new rules. Every time I see the two of you starting to get back at each other for something, I'm going to watch for who started the problem, or who tried to get even first. That boy will get a consequence—maybe no TV or computer for a day. If both of you are at fault, you'll both get a consequence. If you try to solve the problem in a friendly way yourselves, there will be no consequence. Also, if you come to me or your mother and ask for help in solving a problem *before* trying to get back at each other, there will be no consequence for whoever comes to us. Any questions?"

This method of dealing with sibling revenge-seeking creates a built-in incentive for these brothers to seek help in resolving their conflicts. Now, suppose Mike comes to Dad and complains that Bobby was running through the living room and stepped on his toy car. Because it was an accident, Dad responds as follows: "I know it upsets you that your car is broken, and I'm very proud of you for coming to me first instead of fighting with your brother. Do you think you can go back to playing with him now, or would you like me to help you talk with him?"

If Mike expresses the need for help, and it's clear that the toy-breaking was an accident, Dad should address the brother as follows: "Bobby, what can you say to Mike that will help him feel better about the car?" If Bobby doesn't apologize, Dad adds, "Suppose I help you. Can you say you're sorry?" If Bobby does, praise him. If he doesn't, Dad imposes a consequence. "I know it's sometimes hard to say you're sorry," he begins, empathically, "but until you do it, you're not going to be able to play any more computer games. I hope you decide to say you're sorry so you can keep playing on your computer, because I know you really like to do that." Continue to enforce the consequence until an apology is made.

Finally, suppose you do not observe the start of a conflict but encounter it in full swing, with each child pounding on the other. In such instances, separate the two children and say, "Both of you must stop right now. If you don't, you will go to your rooms until you tell me that you're ready to be peaceful again, or that you want to come out of your rooms and play by yourselves for a while. When you do start playing together again, if you begin to try to get back at each other, you'll have to play by yourselves the rest of today *and tomorrow*." Notice that the consequence is escalated if the boys continue to battle. When children don't care whether they play together or not, pick a different consequence. If need be, assign a separate, tailored set of consequences to each child.

## "We Were Just Having Fun"

Sometimes siblings, especially boys, will roughhouse, wrestling with each other, rolling around on the ground or the floor. Parents often put an early stop to such boisterous physical play, fearing one child will hurt the other or that the mock conflict will escalate into a real one. "But we were just having fun!" the children chorus.

Parents need to refrain from stepping in if their children rarely end up hurting one another in these jousting matches. Rather, praise them for controlling themselves so that no one gets hurt when they roughhouse. If and when this kind of play does start to get out of control, separate the children and calmly lay down a rule like this one: "I can see that you have fun wrestling with each other, but sometimes it starts to get out of control. I'm afraid it's starting to get out of control now. It's getting too wild and too loud. So from now on, I'm going to tell you to stop no more than two times. If I have to tell you to stop a third time, you'll both go to your rooms for a half-hour. Do you understand the new rule?" Devise whatever consequence you feel will have the desired effect, then enforce it exactly as described. Escalate it if need be. If you end up having to prohibit all aggressive play, so be it. Your children's development will not be inhibited. Kids need to learn that even fun has boundaries.

## Don't Forget to Evaluate Yourself

Finally, try to be more aware of the atmosphere you create in your household. Are you a highly competitive person yourself? Does your own competitive behavior encourage excessive competitiveness in your children? Do you attach more importance to winning than you should? Children sometimes try too hard to win because they see that their parents are hell-bent on winning themselves. Siblings battle to be "first" because, subconsciously, they associate it with currying their parents' approval. Further, mothers and fathers need to guard against comparing their children—as in "Your sister never complains about doing *her* homework!"—or sending messages of favoritism. This can greatly exacerbate sibling rivalry as each child works overtime to win parental love and approval. You are your children's primary adult role model. Responsible parents are never afraid to ask themselves what complicity they may have in their children's provocative behavior.

## Things to Remember About Sibling Rivalry

- ◆ Sibling rivalry is normal and usually healthy, so long as it's kept within reasonable limits.
- ◆ Parents and their children often have very different perceptions of sibling rivalry.
- ◆ When siblings fight, decode the real source of friction between them and respond to the meanings behind their words, not the words themselves.
- ◆ Model calm. If you vent your irritation and frustration, your children will hear only your anger, not the lesson you're trying to teach them.
- ◆ Overreacting to sibling confrontations tends to exacerbate the problem.
- ◆ When siblings fight only rarely, reinforce autonomy in conflict resolution—in other words, stay out of it. Use consequences only when the problem is persistent.
- ◆ Guard against modeling excessive competitiveness. Also guard against comparing your children with one another or exhibiting favoritism.

# The War of Words: Some Case Histories

Throughout this book, I've suggested that one foundation of empathic communication is parents' awareness of, and willingness to change, their own behavior patterns. Children model themselves on the people around them. Provocative behavior almost always has some roots in the behavioral input kids get from other family members, however well meaning it may be. The following case histories—taken from my practice over the years—serve to point out some of the ways in which parents can unintentionally stimulate or exacerbate aggressive or otherwise undesirable behavior in their children. Of course, all names have been changed to protect patients' confidentiality.

## The Wild Child

Jacob, six years old, was more than a handful. I met him early in my career when I was director of training at a mental health clinic affiliated with Los Angeles's Cedar Sinai Medical Center. The boy had already had serious problems in school. The school he was attending currently, his second, referred him to me for evaluation. He was very disruptive in the classroom and had a mouth like a truck driver. When teachers would attempt to give him directions or control him in any way, he would laugh and either ignore them or talk back abusively.

In my first session with Jacob and his parents, everyone spoke at once. It was a chaotic free-for-all of blaming and mutual frustration. Mom was fed up with Dad's lack of patience. Dad was fed up with Mom's permissiveness. Both were fed up with Jacob. A younger sister, three years old, screamed and cried the moment something failed to go her way. The boy played with toys intermittently on the floor, laughed repeatedly at his mother, his father, his sister, and me as well, and informed all of us at one point or another that we were stupid.

It quickly became clear that everyone had to stop talking at once. It was the only way I could retain my own sanity during our sessions, let alone help them restore theirs. So I made a rule, which I knew I couldn't necessarily enforce, that each family member had to finish speaking before anyone else could speak. If anyone rambled away from the central point being discussed at any given moment, I was allowed to intervene and steer the discussion back on track. By slow fits and starts over many weeks, Mom and Dad stopped interrupting one another. The more the parents followed my rule session after session, the more Jacob did, too. I suggested privately to the parents that they ignore outbursts from Jacob during our meetings, whether laughter or name-calling. I also explained Jacob's behavior to him directly. "I can see you're having a very hard time listening to us talk about you," I told him. "I think that's why you keep laughing and acting silly and saying mean things to us, because you hope that will make us stop talking about you." As I mentioned earlier, it's important to share with children your assessment of the meanings behind their words and actions. Little by little, Jacob's use of these attention-getting tactics began to subside. They had ceased to have their old power over the parents, so Jacob started to give them up and calm down a bit.

Over the course of prolonged therapy, this family adjusted its behavior on many levels, and the result was a remarkable improvement in Jacob's behavior and well-being. First of all, Dad was helped to recognize that a significant component of his son's aggressive behavior was modeled on his own style of interaction, especially over the phone. He conducted a lot of business from the home in his son's presence, and he was a brusque, often profane order-giver. His cell phone twittered so constantly during our early sessions that I had to insist he shut it off. Whenever he answered it, he seemed to bark several short instructions and hang up without even saying good-bye. One couldn't help but say to oneself, "Like father, like son."

Dad wasn't happy when I attached some responsibility for his son's behavior patterns to him. But to his credit, he resolved to mend his ways, at least in his son's presence. Meanwhile, Mom constantly became so upset with Jacob that her interaction with him had degenerated into almost nonstop scolding—a litany of "no's" and "don't do that's"—without any real attempts at communication.

On the day that the parents each resolved to make some changes in their own behavior around Jacob, I turned to Jacob and said very gently, "Mom and Dad are going to try not to be so mad at you. They're going to try not to yell at you and to talk with you more quietly. And Jacob, they hope that you will learn not to get so mad, too. You need to learn how to be in better control of the words you use, and you need to follow their rules. If you do, things will go better for you." Jacob replied that he liked to be silly. I responded that it's okay to be silly sometimes, but added that I thought Jacob got silly when someone was telling him something he didn't like or didn't want to hear. "That way, you can just shut off what they're saying," I suggested. Jacob looked down at his lap and started laughing. "See?" I said, smiling. "You're doing it right now, because you don't want to listen to me anymore. But you know what? You did a *great* job of listening to me just now!"

His parents were shocked that Jacob had paid as much attention as he had. It was clear that I was simply the first person in a long time who had spoken to the boy in such a calm, reassuring tone of voice. More important, he had taken in his parents' expressed willingness to change their own behavior. Most children rarely see their parents admit to being wrong. So it should come as no surprise that they, too, can be resistant to amending their ways. Further, Jacob's parents had, to a considerable degree, "given up" on the boy. They had ceased to establish and consistently enforce rules because they so dreaded their child's aggressive responses to them. It was all too unpleasant, so they had fallen into a habit of leaving Jacob alone and letting him do as he pleased.

At the end of one memorable session, I asked Jacob to

put away the toys he had strewn all over the floor. He flatly refused, telling me to put them away myself. "No," I said calmly, "you'll have to put them away before you can leave." The parents chimed in angrily, "Put them away *now*, Jacob!" He again refused. I signaled to the parents to say nothing and wait it out. Jacob became very agitated and shouted (and I quote!), "Goddamn it, you bastard, I have an important phone call to make!" Like father, like son again. Very quietly, I said, "Jacob, you can't always be the boss. I'm going to help you learn that it's better to follow some rules that I'm going to teach your mother and father." Jacob continued to resist, calling me and his parents unprintable names. But at last he gave in. It took nearly a half-hour, but Jacob grudgingly put the toys back in the box when he saw that he wasn't going to leave until he did. "Jacob," I said, "you made a good decision. See you next week." Incredibly, the boy gave me a hug. His parents were dumbstruck. The truth was that Jacob *wanted* limits. All children do. When rules are defined and enforced in firm but caring ways, they become more, not less, compelling. I don't mean to imply with this brief description of Jacob's sessions that his problems evaporated overnight. It took two years of individual therapy, a special school program, and many separate sessions with the parents. Jacob's mother and father learned more empathic, calm, and patient modes of communication and encouraged changes in their son's behavior by employing incentives and consequences consistently. They spent as much time and effort analyzing and amending their own behavior patterns as they did working with Jacob. But the results made it all worthwhile. Jacob entered a normal third grade and did fine.

## Pooped

Marshall's parents were exhausted. At their pediatrician's recommendation, they came to me for help with their five-and-a-half-year-old because he was still wearing pull-ups. To borrow his family's terms for it, he refused to poop in the potty. He was also verbally provocative and disobedient. When the children in his kindergarten teased him for smelling bad, he would punch them.

Both parents seemed to have very ineffective parenting styles. Dad would give up on Marshall easily, rolling his eyes and walking away when the boy misbehaved. Mom would put up with all she could stand, then finally blow her stack. Only then would Marshall pay attention—briefly.

During one session, the boy declared that he wasn't going to start pooping in the potty until he was ten because he could drive everyone crazy until then. He was clearly succeeding. I began by insisting that the parents stop putting pull-ups on the boy immediately. If he made a mess in his pants, it was his problem and his alone. He would have to take a shower, then wash his clothing in the bathtub himself. This rule was to be enforced without capitulation or compromise. After several "accidents" and the ensuing showers and wash sessions, Marshall started using the toilet.

As in the previous example, overall improvement in Marshall's behavior didn't happen overnight. The sessions I had with the family revealed several parental behavior patterns that this willful child used to accumulate power, which he wielded expertly. The father habitually left disciplinary issues to his wife. He would make vague threats that he almost never followed through on, like "If you don't stop this you're going to be in big trouble!" Such rejoinders are far too unspecific to hold much weight with a child, who will invariably keep testing the limits, inch by inch. In short, Dad was "cowed" by Marshall. The boy had won. He had more power over his father than his father had over him, and he knew it. Mom was tougher on Marshall than her husband was, and she tried sporadically to put limits on the boy's behavior. But her efforts were uneven, and she never had Dad's consistent participation. In the absence of any concerted, organized program of discipline, Marshall became extraordinarily adept at getting his way in the end. The father's ongoing message in the household was "I don't want to deal with it." The mother's was, "I can be pretty tough, but if you're persistent enough, you can wear me down."

In a series of sessions, I worked with both parents to devise a disciplinary system in which everyone would participate every day. Dad had to get more involved in controlling Marshall's provocative behavior. Mom became more aware of how and when Marshall was still dominating her. She learned how to give less power to her son's misbehavior by remaining outwardly calm in the face of it and steadfastly enforcing the rules and consequences that were put in place. Time passed, and Marshall found that his old power plays weren't working the way they used to. As consequences were meted out, agreed upon in advance and enforced by both parents, Marshall started to make "good decisions"—ones his mother and father noted aloud and praised him for. The pull-ups were retired altogether, and Marshall's aggressive behavior began to abate. It was a success story that made everyone feel good, especially Marshall.

## Second Childhood

Patrick and his parents appeared in my office one day. The boy was eight years old and wore a scowl. The father was sixty and acted as if this was the last place on earth he wanted to be. The forty-eight-year-old mother was very serious and intense. I surmised that she had pushed for this session and was bound and determined to make the best of it, uncomfortable as it clearly was for her husband and son.

Patrick had a bad attitude. At least that was how the parents saw it, and it was hard to disagree with them. He was morose and uncommunicative. He displayed clear contempt for both parents and responded to their questions and comments in an annoyed, put-upon tone. Dad had two older daughters from a previous marriage, neither of whom were this troublesome, and whom he loved very much. He was also delighted to have a son and had had high hopes for a mutually satisfying father-son relationship. Patrick was Mom's first and only child. Obviously, both parents had envisioned something far more delightful and gratifying than what they had. The room seemed to fill with stress and toxicity the moment the family entered.

The mother explained that the primary issue was Patrick's attitude toward his father, along with a general temperamental moodiness. As Patrick told me himself, "My dad is so old. I wish I had a younger father like the other kids. Everybody thinks he's my *grand*father!" Dad had no idea how to respond to this. He simply felt hurt and helpless. "How can you talk to your father like that," Mom would scold. "Look at all he does for you! You have no respect for him or anyone!" The mother's oft-reiterated message to Patrick was "you're hurting your father's feelings; you're causing him pain; you're a bad boy." Patrick acted as if he didn't care, but of course he felt terrible inside. He also felt he was always in trouble on this issue, which further alienated him from his father. "Leave me alone," his expression and posture always seemed to say. "Don't talk to me." And Dad was, indeed, in pain, unable to respond to his child's resentments in a way that was helpful to either of them.

This family's "recovery" was a compelling example of the power of empathy. It took many months, but as is always the case in such matters, the time and effort were entirely worthwhile. First of all, Mom had to learn to hear herself more clearly and objectively. At one point she commented to me, "I have so much to give Patrick, but he never makes me feel good." I replied that what she wanted was for Patrick to value her love, and while I certainly appreciated how much she adored her son, it was really not Patrick's job to make her feel loved in return. Far more important, it was her job to help Patrick feel good about himself. And it was clear that Patrick did not feel good about himself. One had the impression he wanted somehow to escape his own skin.

The mother was encouraged to stop making critical comments altogether and to find ways to give Patrick far more positive feedback about himself. Little by little, she began to acknowledge Patrick's feelings in an empathic tone, and to help him work through his resentments at his own speed, not hers. This required from her a level of patience that she had not exhibited in the past. She stopped trying to make Patrick feel guilty and "ungrateful." Rather, she accepted his expressed feelings with empathy, understanding, and concern. She praised the boy for making his feelings known, even when they were troubling to her.

I also urged her to defer to her husband when Patrick

complained about his father's age. It was rightly the father's responsibility to deal with this particular source of friction. Whenever Patrick made a negative age-related comment, Dad would respond along these lines, in a loving, accepting, and confident tone that acknowledged the fundamental normality of Patrick's feelings: "I know you must feel embarrassed and just plain lousy when some kid sees me and asks if I'm your grandfather. If I were you, I'd probably feel the same way. In fact, there have been times when people have come up to me and asked if you were my grandson! But you know what I always say? I say proudly, 'No, that's my son!' And I feel very, very lucky to have you as a son."

As for Patrick, during the sessions I tried to model the kinds of interaction I wanted him to practice as well. I also helped him become more aware of the meanings behind his words. In one of our early meetings, I asked the boy a question, and he looked uncomfortable and annoyed. He refused to answer. In a supportive voice, I said, "I know it's hard to talk. But that's okay. We'll keep trying until it gets easier. Mom and Dad need to learn not to be so mad at you when you don't say things in a friendly way. But it would help if you learn to use friendlier words when you speak. Like, just a moment ago, when your dad asked you about school, you said in a bossy voice 'Stop talking to me!' Instead, could you say, 'Dad, talking about school makes me feel bad,' or 'I don't want to talk about school now, so please don't ask me'?"

After many months of hearing such supportive comments from me and from his parents, Patrick started speaking in friendlier tones. Each time he did, his mother and father praised him for it. They also learned to stop taking Patrick's statements so personally and instead responded empathically to the meanings behind his words, without criticism. Little by little, Patrick became more affectionate and voluntarily spent more and more time with them. Father and son even developed a mutual love of old cowboy movies, which they watched together regularly. Patrick's central problem was not his temperament. It was a need to feel more respect, acceptance, and support from his parents. When they gave it to him, he gave it back. His resentment of his father's age faded, along with his provocative ways.

## Dad in Distress

One day I received a call from the father of a four-year-old girl named Margie. He was frustrated and hurt because his daughter spurned his affections and almost never wanted to be with him, opting instead for her mother, her maternal aunt, or her maternal grandmother. He asked if he could come in alone to talk about whether he was overreacting. We set up an appointment.

This dad adored his little girl, but whenever he so much as kissed her on the cheek, she would wipe it off in disgust. She refused to spend time with him alone, but always insisted on having her mother, grandmother, or aunt present. If they left the room, she would burst into tears! The women gave him frequent suggestions, describing "better ways of doing things." They sincerely wanted to help and offered their suggestions cheerfully, but the father found it all rather humiliating and unpleasant. To him, the message to Margie was "Daddy doesn't know how to talk or play or hug and kiss as well as we do." He had told them how he felt, but they insisted he was being much too sensitive. Margie's mother had been raised almost exclusively by her mother, even though her father was loving and supportive. In the grandparents' older generation, men tended to share less in child-rearing chores, and Grandpa was glad to have his wife look after the kids.

But this younger dad wanted to be much more involved in his daughter's life. He worked long hours, but he dreamed of coming home to Margie's open arms. I asked if there were any occasions when the girl had been more affectionate and accepting of his attentions. He said that the only exception was when he visited her alone at her preschool. There, she sat on his lap, held his hand, and hugged him. He was thrilled, of course, and said he had considered living there instead of at home! To some degree, at least, none of this surprised me, because it's very common for children to go through periods of near-exclusive attachment to one parent or the other. It's a normal developmental phase, and it invariably subsides with time. But in this case, it seemed that some judicious intervention was called for because the father was concerned enough to come to me in the first place, and also because I felt that the adult family members had some complicity in the problem.

I arranged to have all three women of the family join us for the next meeting—Margie's mother, grandmother, and aunt, along with Dad. Fortunately, I had spoken at Margie's preschool, and all of them had attended. They liked what I had said, evidently, and so they readily agreed to meet with me. I gently suggested to the women that they were all such good mothers, they weren't leaving enough room for Dad to be a dad. Margie needed to learn and accept her father's ways as much as she had learned and accepted the women's ways. So first of all, the women had to stop advising him in front of Margie. "Even if it's good advice?" Grandma offered good-naturedly. "Absolutely," I said.

This was a family that had an abundance of attentive, loving mothers. But in a surprising way, it was backfiring at the father's expense. Margie became so narrow in her attachment to the women of the household—all of whom interacted with her in a very similarly attentive manner—that she excluded her father when they were around. When the women offered advice in Margie's presence, however well-meaning, the unspoken message to the four-year-old was "Nobody's quite as good at being with you as Mom/Grandma/Auntie." Dad also complained that whenever he had to set a limit of some kind on Margie's behavior, she would become upset and run to her mother, who would console her with open arms. I urged Mom to avoid involvement in such situations and say instead, "Margie, this isn't a time for a hug from me. This is a time to listen to your daddy and do what he asked you to do. After that, I'll give you a hug."

Similarly, she needed to make frequent comments encouraging and reinforcing Margie's interactions with her father, like, "Daddy can help you with that. I like it when you go to Daddy, because he loves you so much." If Margie resisted, it was agreed that Mom would go with Margie to her father, saying in a calm and soothing voice, "It's nice that Daddy wants to help us, isn't it? We can all do it together." This sharing ritual needed to be carried out again and again, involving Dad in as many familiar household activities as possible.

Whenever Margie spurned her father's affections—by resisting being picked up, for example—I suggested that he try making a bit of a joke of it. He could bend down and quickly kiss the top of her head, for example, then back off, exclaiming, "Gotcha! Boy, I love kissing you!" If she reacted negatively to this, he would simply say in a light tone, "Oh, well, it's okay if you don't want a kiss now," then wait for a later opportunity to give her another quick, lighthearted peck.

I also suggested that Mom tell her husband, privately

and sincerely, that she wanted to do everything she could to encourage Margie to spend more time with him, and that she would request the same commitment from her mother and sister. This would help confirm for the husband that everyone was truly on his side—something I felt he needed to hear.

Finally, I urged the grandmother and the aunt to make it a practice to talk briefly about Dad before he returned home from work every day—for example, about how much he loved her and how anxious he was to get home and see her. Both were instructed to take out a game in advance of the father's return every few days and say to Margie, "Daddy wants to play this game with you when he gets home!" The women readily agreed.

A couple of months later, I learned that the situation had improved markedly and that Margie had gone on her first overnight trip with her father. This family's good-natured willingness to look at themselves and modify their behavior brought about a quick and happy ending to the story. Had they not been so cooperative, the problem would likely have subsided eventually, but certainly not as rapidly.

## Cody and the White-Coated Monster

A worried mother called to report that her four-year-old son, Cody, was having recurrent nightmares. She had asked him if he wanted to talk with someone about them, and he had said yes. So an appointment was set up, and her precocious little boy immediately related to me a terrifying chase that he had dreamed about repeatedly. "A monster in a white coat" was at his heels, intent on "doing something bad" to him. Cody was very advanced verbally, and his description of this scary vision was remarkably detailed, supported by vivid hand gestures and even sound effects.

I questioned the mother about her activities in the last several months. She revealed that she had had an operation and was hospitalized for a week. Cody had visited her there repeatedly, so she found it hard to believe that he could have found the experience particularly traumatic. However, as I interacted further with Cody, it became clear that he had not fully understood why his mother had gone away, nor that she was going to come home again after a short absence. In his mind, the white-coated people he saw at the hospital had taken his mother away from him, were preventing him from being with her as much as he wanted to, and would not necessarily allow her to come back to him.

I include this brief story to suggest how easily one can assume too much about a small child's understanding of a relatively common life experience. This devoted mother hadn't made it clear enough to her son that the doctors and nurses in all those strange white coats were going to help her get well, that they were all friends and not gatekeepers bent on keeping her separated from her child. Empathy means not only sympathy and consideration, it also means remembering at all times that young children lack the tools and experience to understand things the way adults do. Very often, our grown-up point of view causes us to assume unwittingly that a child comprehends far more than he actually does. One must listen very carefully for the signals children give about what they do and don't understand.

## The Story of Anne—a Failed Case

"My daughter's about to be expelled from her private school," said a mother to me over the phone one day. "They're telling me that if I don't get professional help for her, it's all over. The whole thing's ridiculous, but I'm calling you. What choice do I have?" I met with the mother alone first and learned that her seven-year-old second-grader, Anne, cried inconsolably much of the day in school, became extremely upset if the slightest thing went wrong, and constantly asked to be picked up early and taken home by her mother. The teachers had tried their best to deal with the problem but without success. Now, push was coming to shove.

Anne was conceived by artificial insemination. The forty-five-year-old mother had never married and had lived with her own mother until she was about thirty. She had a large trust fund and had never needed to work, so her baby became the total focus of her life. I say this nonjudgmentally; these were simply the facts of the case. The mother had read extensively on parenting and considered herself very knowledgeable about child rearing, which, in many ways, she was. In her view, the school simply did not understand Anne or how to interact with her. She had had many disagreements with the teachers and administrators, and she rejected the possibility that her daughter had any genuine emotional problems. I sensed that this could be a difficult case, even at this early stage, because the mother seemed so rigidly convinced that the school was the sole source of the difficulty.

Over the course of the next several months, I met with the mother and child together on repeated occasions and also had the opportunity to observe them together in group parenting sessions. It was clear that the seven-year-old suffered from unusually serious separation anxiety. It was equally clear that the mother felt that she, herself, was all the company her daughter needed. Anne had never gone on a play date—her mother didn't consider them necessary or even advisable. In the group parenting sessions, mother and daughter interacted and amused each other alone. In fact, the mother tended to be critical of the other parents and their kids afterward. Her constant message to her daughter, in a variety of unspoken ways, was "We don't need anyone else." Anne lacked social skills and quickly seemed overwhelmed when other children got near her. To make matters worse, whenever Anne would make a comment to me, her mother would restate to me in her own words what the little girl had just said. I called her attention to this, and she replied defensively that Anne couldn't always explain what she wanted to say, that there was nothing wrong with helping her.

This kind of relationship is referred to in my profession as "fusion of mother and child." Anne was not being allowed to develop a sense of self, to grow in her own unique way. Her mother's monopolization of her life, while motivated by love, was seriously impeding her social development. The greatest challenge proved to be helping the mother to recognize this and accept it. I tried to be as diplomatic as I could, validating her feelings whenever it seemed appropriate. But despite my best efforts, Anne's mother seemed more and more threatened every time I delicately offered her a suggestion. She was not ready to acknowledge that her daughter needed a life outside of her circle of influence, and became more and more critical of the school and its faculty. She also began to express doubts that I appreciated Anne's uniqueness. Finally, she called and terminated therapy, telling me that she had removed her daughter from the offending private school and was moving away. That was the last I ever heard from her.

I include this story to suggest yet another way in which parents can unwittingly promote and perpetuate provocative behavior in their children. In Anne's case, I'm applying the term *provocative* rather loosely—she was not aggressive, but her upsets at school certainly provoked serious reactions from her teachers. The mother's lack of objectivity about herself, her unwillingness to change, and her uncommon need to keep Anne a little girl who only needed her mom and no one else, had lamentable consequences for the child.

## Things to Remember

- ◆ The lesson in all these stories is that parental self-awareness is a cornerstone of empathic communication. The examples we set in our children's lives are the most powerful behavior modifiers of all.
- ◆ I hope also that these stories help you decide when and if you will seek professional assistance yourself. Obviously, the people whose cases I have described decided to consult a psychotherapist, and I think most would agree that the results were positive. You may feel that you'd like to try the suggestions contained in this book first before taking any further action. That's fine, too. As I said at the outset, I can't possibly address every situation or need in these pages. You'll have to be the judge of whether you can handle your parenting challenges alone, or whether you need outside help. This issue is discussed in greater detail in Chapter 15.

# Just When You Think You've Seen Everything

I've been a practicing child psychologist for many years now, and as I'm sure you can imagine, I've encountered my share of odd behaviors in my patients. In this chapter, I'll describe a few of them. All of these cases are instructive despite their offbeat nature. Do you see something of the spirit of your own child here? Something of yourself? If nothing else, you may come away reassured that your kids aren't as unusual as you thought! Once again, the names are fictitious, but the stories themselves are true.

## Jarod the Fake Spitter

This otherwise charming five-year-old inexplicably started approaching his parents and grandparents, puckering his lips, and making a guttural sound as if he were about to spit on them. Understandably, all the other family members warned him on these frequent occasions that he'd "better not!" At one point, Grandma even looked all over her lap and checked her face to see if the boy had actually spat on her. Jarod seemed to love this, laughing uproariously.

The mother, whose husband is a good friend, called me and asked for advice. I suggested that the family's reaction to Jarod was perpetuating the problem. All the boy wanted was attention—an entirely normal need—and he discovered that threatening to spit on people worked beautifully. I urged her to stop reacting altogether, and to tell everyone else in the household to do the same. From that point forward, every time Jarod threatened to spit, everyone acted like he wasn't even in the room. They continued their conversations, went on with their reading and TV-watching, and so forth. After a day or two of this, Jarod tried announcing his intent: "Look! I'm going to spit on you!" Still no reaction. Later the same day he exclaimed, "You're not doing this right!" Everyone in the room had difficulty stifling laughter, but they controlled themselves. The behavior was gone within a week. As we've seen in some of the other cases described in this book, parents sometimes perpetuate undesirable behavior simply by reacting to it.

## The Boy on the Leash

Early in my career a mother who had recently divorced was referred to me. Her five-year-old, Joey, reportedly refused to follow directions. They lived in a small one-bedroom apartment, I was told, and Joey slept on a cot, which he said he liked. Mother and son socialized very little and were alone together most of the time. The first time they appeared in my office, Joey wore a harness to which his mother had attached a long leash. I was rather startled by this, but managed to maintain a professional, neutral manner. Why, I asked her matter-of-factly, did she keep Joey on a leash? She explained that if she took it off outside, he would run away down the street. If she took it off in my office, he would bolt out of the room and hide. Joey grinned as his mother described the problem. "But the reason I'm here," she continued, "is because of what started last week. I was on the sidewalk with Joey, and suddenly he started crawling on all fours and barking like a dog at the people we passed. He lifted his leg by a tree. One man said, 'Nice doggie' to him, and Joey acted like he was sniffing his leg. It was so embarrassing I'm afraid to take him out of the house anymore. I've yelled at him and pleaded with him to stop, but he won't."

This was an instance in which the five-year-old's behavior was no more unusual than the parent's. Clearly, the boy was behaving like a dog because his mother was treating him like one. I suggested an immediate end to the leash, along with a set of incentive-and-consequence strategies to wean Joey from his habit of running away from his mother. This behavior, along with the dog impersonation, was simply the boy's way of getting attention. The impulse is completely normal, though the manner in which some children act it out can become problematical. And of course, the mother exacerbated the problem by attempting to control her child in inappropriate ways. In a few weeks, Joey's runaway habits began to improve, and he was untethered to boot.

## The Blabbermouth

Kelly was an extraordinarily verbal five-year-old who developed a novel and highly effective strategy for getting her parents' attention and exercising power over them. She blabbed about private family matters. Some sample comments:

> *To a store clerk:* "Did you know that my mommy and daddy were screaming at each other last night?"
> *To her father's parents:* "Mommy once punched Daddy in the arm when she was mad at him. She did it another time, too!"
> *To the parents of a schoolmate:* "My daddy farted last night. It smelled so bad I screamed."
> *To her father's boss:* "Daddy said you were a jerk."

Kelly didn't fully understand what made these comments so upsetting to her parents, but she loved their panicky reactions, and so she refused to stop. It was all her way of flexing her muscles. Fortunately, Dad didn't lose his job, and Kelly was persuaded to be more discreet after some new empathic incentives were introduced. Mom and Dad learned to tone down their reactions to Kelly's comments so they lost their attention-getting power. They also learned to be far more careful about what they discussed within earshot of their daughter!

## The Nose Picker

Nickie, eighteen months old, became such a dedicated nose-picker that his parents called me for help. He would excavate for a while, study the results, then wipe them on whatever was handy, from his shirt to the kitchen table leg. It didn't stop there, though *you* may want to. Next came the eating. And the showing what was in his mouth to everyone. Anyway, you get the idea.

Predictably, the parents reacted to this with horror and revulsion. Nickie quickly learned that the fastest way to get a rise out of Mom and Dad was to stick his finger up his nose and display whatever he found as conspicuously and insistently as possible. As in some of the previous examples, the key to discouraging this toddler's behavior was to refrain from reacting to it. After a while, as Nickie found that his nose-picking no longer garnered the old, horrified reactions, he gave it up.

## The Collector

Bruce, age four, adopted a strange hobby: He collected napkins. At the end of every meal, at home or away, he would grab all the used paper napkins off the table. At first, his parents thought it was cute. But as a pile of more than thirty napkin-filled plastic bags accumulated in the corner of his room, Mom and Dad became concerned. Bruce screamed and cried if anyone tried to put a stop to his napkin-collecting or urged him to throw his treasure trove away.

When I first met the parents, I asked them why they

hadn't simply put their feet down and discarded the napkins. They replied that this would have brought on a huge tantrum from the boy. I replied that they were probably right, but that obviously the napkins needed to go. So I suggested that they give Bruce an early warning. Following my advice, they told him that the following Monday morning—three days away— a new rule would go into effect. All the napkins had to go except for one bag, and there could be no more collecting after that. "We know that may be something that will be hard for you to do at first," they said, supportively, "but we know you can learn to stop collecting napkins." I also suggested that the parents offer Bruce the option of putting the napkins in a recycle bin so they could have "a new life" somewhere else. He could also be shown an example of something made from recycled paper.

Predictably, when Mom and Dad broke the news to Bruce, he threw a tantrum. But the parents remained firm, and on the appointed day, they carried out the plan. Bruce put his collection in a recycling bin and gave up his hobby for good.

Children love to collect things, and Bruce simply made a rather offbeat choice when he decided what he wanted to collect. To Bruce, the napkins were his first stash of "special treasures." They also got him favorable attention. Nearly everyone, except his parents, found it cute and funny. Further, collecting the napkins was Bruce's first "job," and he was the occupation's only practitioner. When seen from this more childish perspective, it all seems to make a bit more sense, doesn't it? Unfortunately, the collection was probably a health hazard, too, so its days had to be numbered. These parents were a little too reluctant to upset their son. He got over it!

## Things to Remember

♦ Children are inexperienced human beings, and we shouldn't be too surprised when they do things that seem extraordinarily odd or ill-advised. They're simply experimenting, or they're displaying a normal need for attention.

♦ Young children don't differentiate clearly between positive and negative attention. *Any* reaction is good as far as they're concerned. It makes them feel more powerful. So parents need to guard against perpetuating undesirable—even bizarre—behavior by protesting it too vociferously.

♦ Kids are remarkably resilient. Setting firm limits, using the empathic methods I've outlined, can still elicit highly emotional reactions from children, but they invariably recover their equanimity quite soon and are none the worse for the experience. In fact, they come to learn that they feel more comfortable and safe when appropriate behavioral boundaries have been set.

# 14

# Provocative Communication and the Media

**M**uch controversy surrounds the issue of the media's effects on children. Does the proliferation of hyperactive, often violent imagery on television and computer screens stimulate aggressive impulses in viewers? I believe it sometimes does. My many years of experience as a child psychotherapist have suggested this to me again and again. The children of belligerent, provocative parents are more likely to display those attributes themselves, and it's logical and likely that such behavior is more imitative than inherited. Children are impressionable. They take in what they see and echo it in a variety of ways. All of us have observed this countless times. So to my mind, it's rather silly to suggest that television somehow manages to sidestep all the imitative phenomena we so often observe elsewhere in children's lives.

Before the various modern media were invented, kids used their imaginations to create aggressive fantasies. And imagination has its own, built-in brakes. A child creates in his mind only that which he can handle, only that which satisfies his personal needs at that moment. Even radio, which certainly had its share of violent, frightening dramas, required the listener to do all the visualization. In their minds' eyes, younger audience members made the villain only as scary-looking as *they* wanted, not as the director or producer wanted.

Early movies sanitized violence and aggression. Even Alfred Hitchcock never actually showed the knife plunging into Janet Leigh's flesh in that famous shower scene in *Psycho*. But today, motion pictures have ceased to leave anything to the imagination. Everything, no matter how lurid or disturbing, is shown in unflinching detail. And let's face it, it's much harder to shut off these images than it is to shut off our imaginations. Lurid, violent imagery has become so ubiquitous that it's all but impossible to completely insulate children from it. Even G-rated advertisements for adult movies are filled with mayhem, and they're everywhere. Once seen, they linger with us, coloring our perceptions whether we like it or not. Many commentators have also complained that the media's definition of acceptable violence for children has become more lax in recent years. Certainly, many of the video games aimed at children feature levels of graphic violence that would have been unthinkable a generation or two ago, and the violence is "interactive"; one can pull the trigger oneself.

To my mind, there are several different issues to consider here. The first is whether viewing violence increases the likelihood that a child will act violently. The second is whether viewing violence numbs children to mayhem, in effect overstimulating them so that they become indifferent to it—an equally undesirable consequence. Finally, television and video games appear to be virtually addictive for many children, which leads one to wonder whether the games themselves actually stimulate addictive behaviors. Might their use lead to other addictions? I believe these are issues worthy of serious discussion.

As the brain grows, it is shaped cognitively and emotionally by both good and bad experiences. What kinds of stimulation, then, should a child's brain receive? When and in what quantities? We all learn from negative as well as positive experiences. Certainly it is valuable for children to experience losing as well as winning. Similarly, it is valuable to experience or at the very least observe sadness and loss. It's all part of growing and learning to function in the real world. But certainly, too, excessive stimulation of certain kinds can become damaging. Real trauma is invariably hurtful to children, and the damage can last for many years. Abuse in the home has similarly dire consequences. Victims of abuse often become abusers themselves, or they become morbidly withdrawn and fearful. Between these extremes of stimulation, where does one draw the line between that which is healthy and that which is dangerous?

The process of socialization—children's interaction with their peers and with adults—is critical. It teaches young people what's appropriate and what isn't, and it stimulates a lot of healthy brain activity involving all kinds of problem-solving. But most parents have seen what can happen when children are overstimulated—let us say by an hour or two of wild, rambunctious play with peers. It can take them quite some time to calm down. They enter the house, their play-time over, and bounce off the walls for a while as their overstimulated brain chemistry slowly returns to normal. Their level of excitation gradually abates, and their usual inhibitions return. So the effects of stimulation do persist well after the source of that stimulation has been shut off. What, then,

can we surmise about exposure to violent images on television and the computer screen? How persistent might the
effects of such exposure be? Do children remain overstimulated after experiencing these "entertainments," or are they
numbed by them? All of this warrants more study, but I
would rather err on the side of caution and rigorously limit
children's exposure to violence on TV, on the computer screen,
and at the movies.

## The Dumbing Down of Our Kids

In a recent scientific study, teachers in the United States and
Europe were asked to assess what differences, if any, they
have observed in their students in the last decade. They
responded that they have noted decreased attention spans,
diminished capacity to stick with a problem, reduced com-
prehension of the complexities of language, and faltering oral
expression and listening abilities. Undoubtedly, many factors
can explain this, but I believe the media need to be less defensive and accept more responsibility for the phenomenon
than they have to date, just as parents need to take greater
responsibility for what their children watch. Today, the aver-
age three- to five-year-old watches some twenty-eight hours
of television a week. Children this age are in their critical
period for cognition and language development. But television requires almost no active participation or self-expression
and tends, by its fundamental nature, to present material in
short, simple "bites" requiring a minimum of sustained attention and critical listening. I include in this description
commercials, which are ubiquitous case studies in linguis-
tic shorthand. One recent study concluded that television

manipulates the brain into paying attention to visual and auditory changes, but in ways that are essentially "unhelpful." In other words, TV (especially children's programming) capitalizes on the brain's involuntary responses to zooms, fast cutting, loud noises, and bright colors, keeping it unnaturally alerted, but at a *responding*, not a *thinking* level. Another clinical experiment demonstrated that children displayed less stick-to-itiveness in tasks like reading and puzzle-solving after they had been shown a fast-paced video.

## Personal Experiences

As I mentioned earlier, again and again in the course of my practice I have encountered the damaging effects of the media on children. Here are several typical examples:

### Jimmy

This generally well-adjusted seven-year-old was given a handheld computer game system for his birthday. At first his parents were delighted with its performance as a "babysitter." It kept Jimmy occupied in the car and entertained him when he accompanied his mother and father on adult errands. But little by little it began to take over his life—so much so that his parents called me to help them wean him from the tiny screen and its little joystick. Jimmy had to have the video game with him virtually all the time. The moment he returned from school, he made a beeline for it and remained under its spell until bedtime. His interest in his friends waned, and he would often sit alone playing with the video game even when surrounded by playmates engaged in activities he used to enjoy. He complained bitterly when his parents tried to limit the game's use, becoming more and more angry and provocative, even physically combative. Clearly, the game had become an obsession. I have seldom, if ever, seen such an intense preoccupation with other kinds of toys in young children. In my experience, video games can have insidious addictive qualities that other forms of children's entertainment simply do not.

## Jane

This five-year-old became as addicted to television as Jimmy was to his handheld video game. It all started innocently enough. Jane started watching TV when she was about three, and her parents were grateful for the respite it provided them in keeping her entertained. But day by day, her mastery of the box's controls and her interest in the televised fare increased. Her parents never set clear limits, so Jane soon spent nearly every free hour in front of the tube. Her social interactions decreased, and she showed little or no interest in any other activities, protesting angrily when her mother and father finally tried to curtail her TV viewing. It took several months of visits to my office and a series of incentive-and-consequence strategies to wean Jane from her habit.

## Donald

This fourteen-year-old attended a prestigious private school on Los Angeles's west side. From the time he was ten, he was his class's resident computer, video game, and Internet expert. He used the computer extensively in his studies, and with excellent results, so his parents were unconcerned, even pleased. But as time went on, Donald became more and more tenaciously glued to the screen. After school, late into the night, and throughout the weekends, he sat in the same place, tapping the keys. His parents became more and more upset, trying in vain to interest him in other pursuits. Donald's refusals to cooperate became, in turn, more and more provocative and profane. His parents characterized this behavior as "very unlike him." Finally, the situation came to a head, and Donald's father entered the boy's bedroom intent on disconnecting the machine altogether. Donald picked up a baseball bat and menacingly ordered his father to back off. Dad threatened to call the police. The boy relented, but the entire family was traumatized and appeared in my office the next day.

Donald was very remorseful about the incident, and together we were able to put in place some new rules about computer usage in the household. But the fact remains that this was an experience foreign to this family. Donald's interest in his computer went well beyond the sort of passion children frequently develop for, say, action figures or baseball cards. His was an addiction that nearly pushed him to lethal violence against his father. I don't mean to suggest that I advocate shielding children from the "evils of technology." Television and the computer are marvelous inventions. But they are also uniquely powerful, sometimes in rather insidious ways, and they demand a special kind of vigilance from parents.

## Things to Remember About Provocative Communication and the Media

♦ Limit children's TV-watching and computer-gaming. I won't presume to say how much of either is enough; each family is entitled to make its own decisions based on individual behavior and need. If you start to feel that your children's "media activities" are occupying excessive amounts of time, or are too often infringing on other, more valuable pursuits, make new rules. Many experts believe that limits should be set based on developmental levels, with small children being allowed less TV and computer time than older kids. Is the child in question gregarious or a loner? The latter might benefit from stronger restrictions on TV-viewing. Use your best judgment, and get advice from teachers and other parents.

♦ Try to stay abreast of ongoing research into the effects of broadcast and computer media on children. This will continue to be a controversial issue, and we should all listen carefully to both sides of every argument.

♦ From the time children are very young, make it clear to them that television viewing and computer time are privileges, and that they will be permitted within reasonable limits based on positive behavior. Excessive use—use that gets in the way of other important or valuable activities—will not be allowed.

♦ Limiting time in front of the TV or computer monitor is just the beginning. Content must be monitored, too. An hour of *Sesame Street* is preferable to three minutes of *Kung Fu Killers from Hell*. Parents must exercise careful and consistent judgment about what is appropriate and inappropriate for their children to see. Go through the TV

(continued)

(continued)

listings. Sample various programs and computer games yourself and decide which ones your kids can have access to and which ones are off-limits. Make lists of the approved shows and games, and enforce the rules you devise. Some young people are more sensitive and impressionable than others, and restrictions must be designed accordingly.

◆ When possible, give children a choice of approved programs they can watch in a given time slot. This helps minimize "the lure of the forbidden" and lets kids feel they still have some power of their own.

◆ The onus remains on parents to function as vigilant and thoughtful filters, ensuring that their children see and experience things that serve their best interests, and shielding them from things that do not.

# Some Q and A's

As one might expect, the parents who schedule appointments with me have many questions. A selection of them follows, along with my answers. Some of the questions deal with commonly seen provocative conduct, others concern more unusual problems. Have your own children ever exhibited behaviors like the ones described?

*My child can be so sweet, and then, suddenly, he blurts out things that make our ears burn! Where do these terrible words and thoughts come from?*

It doesn't register on many parents how much their children take in during every waking moment, even when they don't appear to be listening. Some kids echo what they've just heard immediately, so there's no mistaking where their thoughts and words come from. But others give no inkling of what they have absorbed until it suddenly pops out unexpectedly—like profanity or other harshly provocative words that seem out of character. The source is usually friends, siblings, TV, or the parents themselves. Kids often have a vague sense of what is appropriate to imitate and what isn't, but they frequently misjudge these things and, in a moment of high emotion, let drop a choice four-letter word. It's all part of the learning process, and as any parent knows in this day and age, it's nearly impossible to completely insulate children from profanity and other such undesirable input. If you object to your child's language, begin by watching your own, even when the child is in the next room and seemingly oblivious to you. Kids are sponges that are absorbing more than you think, all the time.

When a young child uses profanity, I recommend saying something like this in a calm tone: "Words like '#@&!!' sound very unfriendly, and grown-ups don't want to hear them. It's better when you use friendly words." Give examples of "friendlier" word choices and praise the child for compliance. When older children use objectionable language around the house, you can employ incentives or empathic consequences as needed to control the behavior.

*Why does my child speak to me in such hate-filled tones and look at me with such hatred in her eyes? Doesn't she love me anymore?*

When preadolescent children—most frequently beginning around age seven or eight—express primitive emotions, like hatred, to a parent, it has nothing to do with loving or not loving that parent. It has to do with their ongoing struggle—and it is a struggle—to learn to delay gratification, to accept criticism, to relinquish their inborn desire for everything to be the way *they* want it to be. It's very, very hard to give up being the center of the universe! Some kids adapt more easily than others. Your job as a parent is to help your children make these difficult transitions by teaching them about themselves and the world they inhabit. It requires enormous empathy and patience.

Remember, also, that children have not yet developed the self-control to keep their harshest thoughts to themselves. All of us have, at one time or another, experienced extreme displeasure with a loved one. Most adults, however, stop short of shouting "I hate you!" at a spouse. Kids lack such self-restraint. So don't take your kids' nastiest remarks too personally.

*I don't believe my child's provocative comments are "unintentional." My child knows exactly what he's saying to me.*

When children are provocative, their own, raw feelings come first, and they do not understand the roots of those feelings in any truly helpful way. The capacity for real self-understanding and logical, rational communication takes a long time to develop. A five-year-old may declare, "I said that to you because I was mad at you," but this is a kind of self-awareness that is still rather fleeting and not at all thought out. All of us, even as adults, sometimes blurt out hurtful statements that we later regret to partners, family members, or friends. We are often not even conscious of our own deeper motives. Imagine how hard it must be for a grade-schooler.

Just the same, there are times when children are, indeed, aware that their comments are likely to provoke their parents. They are either testing their limits, or they lack the communication skills to say what's really on their minds. In these situations, parents should try to decode what's really going on and share their conclusions with the child. For example, say, "Honey, I think you may be saying unfriendly things to me because you're bored and want to get my attention. Maybe next time you can say something like, 'Mommy,

I don't have anything to do. Can you please play with me?' That would be much better."

*Why does my child only behave provocatively toward me? He doesn't talk that way to his friends or teachers or grandparents.*

Often, the parent who does the most for a child is at the receiving end of most of the aggressive and regressive behavior. Kids feel the safest and most secure with the parent they perceive as most attentive through thick and thin. "You are the person to whom I have learned to come first whenever I have a need," children feel. Since they are not yet good at deferring gratification, this person becomes the brunt of their frustration when their needs are not met.

To be sure, some parents inadvertently reinforce the very behaviors they resent in their children, as we have seen elsewhere in this book. But if your child seems to take aim at you more than anyone else, it's likely because he feels more dependent upon you than anyone else.

*Where and how can children learn that being mean to someone else hurts feelings and isn't nice?*

Preschool kids begin to learn about empathy largely from the adults around them. Their ability to perceive another child's displeasure doesn't go far beyond observing whether there are tears or not. It's up to adults to say, "That's not nice. You'll hurt your friend's feelings." As children get older, they become more aware of the subtleties of emotion and are better able to put themselves in someone else's shoes, assuming parents and other caregivers model and facilitate it. They develop deeper kinds of caring about their friends and hence feel greater concern about alienating them. In parallel, their peers are now quite capable of saying things like "Stop being mean to me." By applying the lessons outlined in this book and modeling empathy more consistently and effectively yourself, you can accelerate your child's acquisition of empathy for others.

*When my child is being nasty to me, I find myself not liking him and wishing I had a different child. Is there something wrong with me for feeling that way?*

No. All of us, adults and children alike, harbor primitive feelings and thoughts when we are under stress. Very often, these primitive feelings are directed at those we love and care about the most. What matters is how we behave. Obviously, one shouldn't communicate such thoughts to a child, either directly or indirectly.

*What's so awful about an occasional spanking? My parents spanked me and I turned out all right.*

I've made clear my feelings about corporal punishment elsewhere in this book, but the subject is worth touching upon once again. Certainly, many recipients of numerous childhood spankings have "turned out fine." But physical punishment remains "government by fear." It is a parental temper tantrum, and kids know this. It leaves children with mixed messages about love and about getting along with others: "I love you, except sometimes I get so angry at you I hit you," "Hitting is a way of controlling smaller, weaker people," and "You're not allowed to hit others, like your brother or sister, but I am allowed to hit you." In this book, I am proposing discipline *without anger*. It's very difficult. Readers used to shouting at their recalcitrant children will find it very, very hard to stop. But squelching provocative behavior and language with loud scoldings and physical punishment teaches children nothing about themselves, nothing about their own hostilities and frustrations and how to deal with these strong emotions more constructively. As a parent, ask yourself, do you want to teach your children something, or do you just want to control them?

*Will my child always be this difficult, or will she grow out of it?*

Yes. I'm being ambiguous for a reason: Small children who become enamored of talking about, say, toilet issues invariably grow out of it as their preoccupations change with time. Bossy, excessively demanding children tend to develop better communication skills as they mature, and their bossiness subsides naturally. Even children whose natural temperaments are moody, persistent, reactive, and so forth, can change their ways with proper guidance. However, children who grow up in families that model aggressive communication and behavior tend to retain those traits, even into adult life. So yes, there is always hope, but sometimes the greatest hope hinges on parents' willingness to analyze and amend their own styles of interaction with each other and with their children.

*Some families scream and yell at each other all the time, yet it always seems to blow over, and in many ways they're devoted to one another. What gives?*

It's true that some families are very passionate and emotional, let their feelings out vociferously, and yet profess sincere love for one another. "We just fight to get it out of our systems," they say. "We don't take it personally. When it's over, we're all fine in five minutes, and life goes on." Just the same, in my experience I would say that such families cheat themselves and each other out of more meaningful and satisfying forms of conflict resolution. There is a tendency to affix blame to others and never to look at oneself, so problems are not resolved to the extent they might be. Resentments brew and can manifest themselves later, sometimes after many years. I suspect that family members who behave this way are not as close to one another as they may think.

*Every time my four-year-old sees my mother, she tells her to go away. If her Grandma kisses her, she wipes it off. This is terribly embarrassing for me. What can I do?*

Regardless of how this particular behavior got started, the likelihood is that the grandmother now makes it known, through a variety of cues, that she is displeased with it. She may act hurt when the child rejects her, or she may complain to the mother within the girl's earshot. If the four-year-old could explain herself, she might say, "Grandma's no fun. She gets me into trouble with my mom, who pressures me to let Grandma kiss me. And when she does kiss me, it's wet and yucky. That's why I wipe it off. I wish Grandma would stay away from me altogether."

What to do? I told the mother to ask Grandma to refrain from kissing the girl, and from asking for kisses from her, for the time being. The child just wasn't quite ready for it. Alternatively, if Grandma asked for a kiss and was rejected, I suggested that she respond, in a friendly, positive tone, "It's okay if you don't want to kiss your grandma. I'll always love you anyway." At the same time, Mom was urged to say to the four-year-old, before Grandma's arrival,"If Grandma asks for a kiss, you can tell her, 'No, thank you, Grandma, but I still love you.' If you can do that, it would be great! And please don't tell her to go away when she visits us. That makes her think you don't like her. Maybe you can ask her to come play with your toys with you. I'll come, too." She added an incentive as well: "If you can do this, we'll have an extra story before bedtime tonight." Generally, situations like these don't require consequences.

*My three-year-old is afraid of anyone with dark skin. He cowers behind me in the presence of African Americans and won't come out. This is mortifying to me.*

This child probably lacked sufficient exposure to children of ethnicities other than his own. It is also possible that some isolated incident or overheard comment elicited the behavior. Whatever the case, I suggested that the mother obtain some children's books about people of different ethnicities—there are plenty in any public library—and read them to her son. Some multicultural dolls or other toys could prove helpful. So, too, would joining a playgroup or attending an activity that brought the child into informal contact with a broader spectrum of people.

*My five-year-old drops his pants and exclaims, "Look at my big butt!" He finds this hilarious. At first, I did, too, but it's not funny anymore. He won't stop!*

Four- and five-year-olds are just beginning to become aware of their body parts and sexual identities. They're also developing a sense of humor. This boy may have seen an older sibling or playmate bare his behind, and hilarity probably ensued. To boot, Mom laughed, too, at least at first. I told her to stop laughing, of course. The second step was to install a consequence—in this case, an earlier-than-usual bedtime every time the pants dropped. They stayed up.

*My eight-year-old daughter is sometimes verbally provocative. When I reprimand her and threaten a consequence, she begs for forgiveness and promises she'll never do it again. She keeps her promise for a few days, but then the provocative behavior comes back.*

Whether consciously or unconsciously, many children become extremely adept at outmaneuvering their parents. Again and again, they manage to slip out of being disciplined. Of course, every time they're successful at evading consequences for their transgressions, they are, in effect, encouraged to continue behaving provocatively.

In this case, I suggested using an incentive to promote better behavior. The mother said to her daughter, "You're a great kid, but I want to teach you to talk friendlier to me and to show what a great kid you are more of the time. So each whole day that you're friendly to me all the time, you'll get a point. If you're unfriendly, I'll remind you about it once, and if you stop being unfriendly right then, with that one reminder, you can still get your point for the day. When you have five points, you can stay up an extra hour on Friday."

The mother used a little chart to keep score, sticking firmly to the new rule without making exceptions or bowing to begging and pleading. She also picked an incentive she knew would be meaningful to her daughter, who loved to stay up late with her older siblings. In this case, the incentive worked. If it hadn't, we would have moved on to consequences.

*My six-year-old son thinks it's a riot to pass gas as noisily as he can. My husband can never keep from snickering when this happens. I don't think it's funny, and I can't get him to stop.*

Reread the pants-dropper episode above! This is a similar behavior. It gets laughs from peers, and even from Dad—what better way to capture attention and show off a new skill? In such situations, and if the problem is only occasional,

I recommend refraining from reacting in any way. If that doesn't put a stop to it within a week or two, then install a consequence that can be escalated if necessary: the conspicuous passing of gas means an early bedtime!

*My nine-year-old daughter thinks she's my mother. She advises me on fashion, on how I fix my hair, on what to buy for the house. She analyzes my friends and even offers opinions on which of them are best for me. The thing is, most of the time, I can't disagree with her. She's usually right! But it's driving me nuts!*

This was a very precocious child, both intellectually and emotionally. As a result, her parents had quite naturally given her considerable power and independence in the household. They involved her in many adult activities, where she was a welcome addition, admired by all. With all the best intentions, they had encouraged what had now become a rather unpleasant trait in their daughter: She was overstepping her bounds and offering her opinions when they weren't welcome. The mother, too, was somewhat lacking in self-esteem, which further complicated the problem.

In my experience, when children are encouraged to act like adults too early—as this little girl had been, however innocently—they frequently begin to have trouble in their relationships with peers, who see them as bossy, controlling, or just plain odd. Kids need to be kids. In this instance, I encouraged the mother to start treating her daughter more like a nine-year-old, and less like a grown-up companion. I suggested she say something like the following, in a friendly but firm voice: "Honey, from now on I will let you know when I want your opinion on my clothes or anything else. If you start telling me what I should do, I'll remind you that I'm going to make my own decision. It's my job to help you make decisions; it's not your job to make my decisions for me." Her day-to-day message to her daughter needed to be: "I am entirely capable of taking care of myself. If I need your help, I'll ask for it." After a number of these reminders over several weeks, the girl stopped offering so many opinions. She also became more appropriately separated from her mother and other adults—an added benefit that would likely enhance her relationships with her peers.

*My daughter, age five, makes embarrassing statements to my mother and father. She told them they smell funny. She asked my father why he has so much hair in his ears and nose. She's an acute observer of imperfections, and when she finds one, she lets the owner know about it; not rudely but as a statement of fact. My parents are upset about it, and it makes me feel uncomfortable because I think they consider me a poor disciplinarian.*

This five-year-old's behavior was a normal expression of curiosity about people's similarities and differences. Children are acutely observant—it's how they learn. This mother was instructed to talk with her daughter prior to the grandparents' next visit, using words like these: "Honey, I know you're interested in things like how Grandma and Grandpa smell and whether they have hair in their ears, but Grandma and Grandpa really don't like it when you ask questions about things like that. It makes them feel bad, even though they know you don't mean to make them feel bad. So I hope you can remember not to ask Grandma and Grandpa questions about things like that. I'll bet you can. Ask Mommy, instead, when Grandma and Grandpa aren't here." Most children respond readily to requests like this one. This girl's behavior improved after a few such reminders. Had it not, incentives and consequences would have been employed.

*How can you tell when a child needs professional help?*

Most parents turn to professionals after they have "tried everything" themselves and failed to bring about any improvement in their child's behavior. This may be your first parenting book, or it may be your tenth. I hope it's your last and that it helps you. But if it doesn't, if you feel that your child's provocative behavior is unrelenting and excessive, you may benefit from outside intervention. Also, it is important to evaluate your child's general demeanor apart from the provocative behavior. If he or she seems unhappy in general, withdrawn and disinterested, then depression could be part of the problem. If this is the case, a professional can offer a great deal of help.

Other signals that professional intervention may be in order include unwillingness to accept or discuss any blame or responsibility for words or actions, and recurrent regression, including helplessness and frequent or inappropriate crying. If your child exhibits any of these behavioral traits, would you classify them as mild, moderate, or severe? It's not often the easiest of judgment calls.

Consider this example:

Michael was eight years old and functioned well on many levels. But he was extremely rigid and required things to be done in very particular ways. He followed rules obsessively, and when peers broke the rules, especially while playing sports at school, he became extremely upset and withdrew angrily. He could not tolerate teasing of any kind and seemed to take everything too seriously. He was spending more and more time sulking on the sidelines, frustrated with everybody and everything. His teachers and parents were unsuccessful at bringing about any improvement. In general, this child was not developing appropriate coping skills. He was professionally evaluated, and individual and family counseling were prescribed, with good results.

Michael's difficulties could have been written off as moodiness or oversensitivity. He wasn't provocative in any classic way, spouting curses or lashing out physically. But his caregivers made a thoughtful judgment call, sought outside help, and benefited substantially.

Finally, don't neglect to evaluate yourself as well. Are you at the end of your rope? Does your child's behavior push you to tears or to physical violence? Sometimes the parent needs, and can benefit from, expert support just as much as the child, even when the behavior problems in question aren't all that severe or unusual.

If you suspect that intervention may be in order, schedule a preliminary consultation with a qualified professional. Such a practitioner should tell you if therapy is, indeed, called for and explain why in a clear, convincing way.

*Whom should I call?*

Developmental pediatricians, child psychologists, and child psychiatrists can all help. I urge people to find someone who has real expertise in parenting issues as well as child psychology. Such therapists, by definition, have an in-depth understanding of developmental psychology, which means they will know whether your child's behavior is age-appropriate or not. They will also be able to offer practical, day-to-day advice on how you can respond to the difficulty. Also important is the ability of the therapist to talk with you about your communication with the child, the extent to which you hear and respond to your child's expressed and unexpressed feelings, and the meanings behind his or her words. The difficulty doesn't always emanate exclusively from the child, so individual therapy may address only part of the problem. More often than not, parents need to be fully involved in the process, too.

*Where can I get a name?*

From trusted friends, relatives, schools, pediatricians, and other family doctors. Avoid blind searches in the Yellow Pages. Most therapists are reputable and qualified, but some are not, and a referral is the best course. Sometimes I receive calls from parents who have observed improvement in another child, and then learned that that child had been seeing me. So be watchful and do some homework before making that appointment. Look for therapists with the special qualifications described in the previous answer. Don't be afraid to quiz people thoroughly about their suggestions. Insist on a thoughtful reply. Do they know anything about the practitioner's background? What has particularly impressed them? Assuming they know a patient in the practitioner's care, what improvement have they observed and how long did it take? Did the practitioner offer parenting advice as well as advice to the child?

If all else fails and you are unable to obtain a referral, then it's worthwhile to contact a nearby university. Of course, there are no guarantees, but in my experience, therapists who are affiliated with universities tend to be well-qualified and experienced. Local help lines can also be valuable resources, because they're usually manned by volunteers who have personal experience with the professionals they recommend.

Once you have selected a therapist, don't be afraid to ask him or her plenty of questions, too—about training, philosophy, treatment approaches, and so forth. Observe the therapist's attitude as he or she answers these questions. Is this someone with whom you feel comfortable? Establishing comfort and trust is one of the most important prerequisites for a successful outcome.

Finally, seeking professional help is a difficult, often painful choice for parents. Many people almost do it, then hesitate for months at a time. Others start seeing a therapist, then drop out, even when their children are beginning to show marked improvement. It's hard to ask for help, to admit to yourself that you need it. It's even harder to admit that your child needs help. For many parents, this is tantamount to an admission of personal failure in a responsibility they consider the most important of their lives. They feel embarrassed and humiliated. Their dreams of experiencing joy and satisfaction in child rearing have been dashed, and they cringe at the thought that something might be wrong with a child they adore. Months, even years, of denial and minimization can further complicate the situation. Parents can feel very resentful of a teacher's urging that their child undergo evaluation. They see it as a personal insult. Often, too, family members will disagree about the severity of the problem. A grandparent may say, again and again, "Oh there's nothing wrong with Jimmy," further complicating the issue. On occasion, different therapists may offer different diagnoses and treatment plans, and in these cases parents tend to favor whichever one is least "serious" and intrusive. The best interests of the child and the family may be compromised.

So it's not easy. But for the parent who has the objectivity and courage to seek help when it seems prudent to do so, there is great benefit to be reaped. The right therapist, in the right setting, can solve—or at the very least greatly ease—most childhood behavioral problems. Parents who seek professional help are not failures. They are, in many ways, the bravest and most caring of all.

## Things to Remember

- As you read the patient anecdotes in this chapter, I hope you were able to anticipate my advice before I gave it. If so, you're well on your way.
- Managing provocative behavior empathically, rather than in anger, needs to become part of your standard vocabulary; it must be second nature to you. That way, you will achieve a new evenhandedness in your interaction with your children, and this consistency will open the door to change.
- When your kids begin to see a reliable connection between what they do and what you do—and a similar strong connection between what you say you'll do, and what you actually do—they will begin to learn new ways of interacting with you, with each other, and with their peers.
- These new ways of interacting will automatically begin to teach your children about the all-important concept of integrity—being a person of your word, taking responsibility for the agreements you make, exercising self-control.
- Real learning and problem-solving simply don't occur when voices are raised. As you learn to control your temper, you'll find that entirely new kinds of "peace initiatives" become possible.
- Asking for professional help is not a sign of weakness, but rather one of strength and responsibility.

# More Humane Parents, a More Humane World

**T**hroughout my thirty years of practice as a child psychotherapist, I have seen a steady, general improvement in parenting skills. I have encountered ever-greater empathy; an ever-greater willingness to challenge older, more punitive parenting methods; and a real desire among parents to build their children's individual identities and self-esteem. To be sure, there are still mothers and fathers who find my ideas too "permissive," but I believe their numbers are dwindling. In fact, my ideas are not permissive at all. I don't believe in permitting aggressive behavior. Rather, I believe in preventing it in ways that do not imitate it.

As I wrote in the first chapter, not that long ago parenting was considered something one should just know how to do. Whatever skills were required were learned from one's own parents. Despite its being one of the most complicated and demanding tasks anyone ever takes on, parenting was not something one studied. Stricter disciplinary practices were also the norm. Provocative behavior was promptly squelched, usually through fear-inducing punishments like spankings. But the fact is, provocative behavior is a normal part of every child's development. However irritating it may be to adults, it performs a variety of critical functions in children's lives. Squelching it teaches nothing and leaves children feeling resentful and misunderstood. Responding to it in measured, caring tones helps kids understand themselves and leaves them feeling acknowledged and valued.

Today's parent is far more educated and effective than the parents of only a few generations ago. Witness the proliferation of books, periodicals, and videos on child rearing. The human race has only developed a theory of child development in the last hundred years. Before Dr. Benjamin Spock's *Baby and Child Care* appeared in 1946, there were no comprehensive resources on parenting skills. So it should come as no surprise that a lot of progress has been made rather recently. A key development in all that progress is that children are no longer expected to behave like miniature adults. For a very long time, this was what punitive, restrictive child-rearing practices sought to create—little grown-ups who were penalized if they dared to behave like children. Today, more and more parents are anxious to raise their kids in humane, supportive ways that acknowledge them for what they are. These parents have moved away from physical punishment and sought instead more instructive and constructive disciplinary methods. They have sought to project their authority in empathic, loving ways that teach their children self-control without impeding their natural development or engendering anxiety and fear.

The more of these parents there are, the better for all of us. We already know that abusive parenting tends to produce future abusive parents. So it's logical that humane parenting will tend to produce more humane grown-ups. Surely the world needs all the humane grown-ups it can get.

# Acknowledgments

I am most indebted to all the parents with whom I have worked over the years. All demonstrated a keen desire to improve their parenting skills, and their inspiring example motivated me to write this book.

I am also eternally grateful to Berea St. John Finer for her many years of support. She has passed her ninetieth year and has a mind and spirit that transcend age and time itself. Thanks as well to my dear wife, Pamela, who continues to put up with me!

I wish to acknowledge two special families that are not only our dear friends but also personify the humane parenting practices I have described throughout this book. The first is Doug and Denise Ross and their terrific son, Jarod. The second is Jim and Tina Huston and their adorable daughters, Lindsey and Taylor.

My thanks to my collaborator, Mark Ritts, for his excellent writing, direction, and editorial assistance on our book. Mark and his wife, Teresa Parente, are also outstanding parents. We both wish to thank Teresa for her repeated readings of the manuscript and her wise and indispensable counsel throughout the project.

My fond regards to the Lupianis. And last, but by no means least, my heartfelt thanks to my agents, B. J. Robbins and Ken Sherman, for the professionalism and expertise that made this book a reality.

# Index

# About the Authors

**Don Fleming, Ph. D.,** brings more than thirty years' experience as a psychotherapist and lecturer to *Mom, I Hate You!* He is the author of two bestselling books, *How to Stop the Battle with Your Child* and *How to Stop the Battle with Your Teenager*. The former was cited by the National Bestsellers Association as one of the top parenting books of the 1990s. Dr. Fleming's articles have appeared in many periodicals, including *Child*, *Working Woman*, and *Working Mother*. Currently, he writes for *Parenting Today's Teens*, a bimonthly newsletter reaching audiences nationwide. Dr. Fleming has been interviewed on many television programs and is a frequent guest on local and national radio shows. He practices psychotherapy in Beverly Hills, California, working with children from two through adolescence, as well as with their families. He also counsels adult individuals and couples. For the first twenty years of his career, he was director of training at the Julia Ann Singer Center, a child psychiatry facility associated with Los Angeles's famed Cedars-Sinai Medical Center. There, he trained interns and residents and ran a treatment program for children who exhibited a wide variety of developmental and behavioral disorders. Dr. Fleming lives in Los Angeles with his wife and colleague, Dr. Pamela Fleming.

**Mark Ritts** has a long and varied background as a writer, producer, director, and performer. His one-hour documentary on microbiology, *Creators of the Future*, recently aired in prime time on PBS. He has created and produced a wide variety of television programs, educational exhibitions, and multimedia presentations for broadcast, corporate, and institutional clients. He was the voice and manipulator of "Kino," the Emmy Award–winning puppet co-host of PBS's *Storytime*, as well as one of the show's writers. He also played "Lester," the guy in the rat suit, on CBS's celebrated science series for kids, *Beakman's World*. A Harvard graduate with a degree in English Literature, Mr. Ritts lives in Los Angeles with his wife, actress Teresa Parente. He has a daughter and two sons, ranging in age from six to twenty-seven.